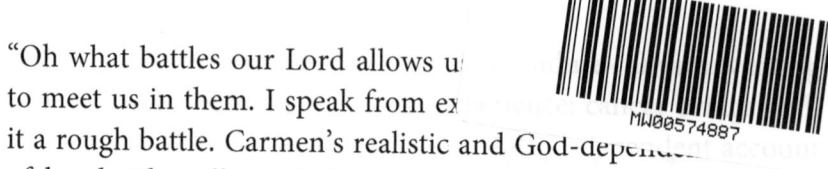

"Oh what battles our Lord allows u: to meet us in them. I speak from ex it a rough battle. Carmen's realistic and God-depend. of her battle will reach deep into the heart of any who share health struggles. A book worth reading whether in good health or poor."

Dr. Larry Crabb
Best-Selling Author, Psychologist,
Founder and Director of New Way Ministries

"You need to read this book. Suffering is the universal lot of fallen humanity. It visits all of us in various forms and degrees. The question is how we deal with it. If we walk through it with our focus on God, it becomes not only tolerable, but a fruitful opportunity. If we focus on our self, it becomes exacerbated with bitterness and misery. Carmen walks us through a most difficult personal battle and shows us how, through the means of God's grace, one can flourish and help others to flourish, even though one is in the deepest and darkest of valleys. Highly recommended."

Dr. Del Tackett
Creator of *The Truth Project* and *Is Genesis History?*
Adjunct Professor, Summit Ministries

"We misconstrue what it means to be weak before God when we liken such weakness to lack of physical strength. Carmen Pate has discovered that the power of God is the greatest strength there is, but that His power is made available to us only when we stop trying to employ our own physical, mental and emotional strength and 'let God.' This is a book that will give hope to and empower many."

Cal Thomas, Syndicated Columnist

"In her candid book, Carmen shares the ups and downs of her medical journey walking through an acute leukemia relapse. Yet Carmen doesn't travel this rocky path alone. With the Lord as her constant companion—instead of being self-focused—we see her focused on meeting and ministering to the needs of others who also need God's powerful strength. As you read her encouraging words, you will be inspired by her story with renewed hope for *your* heart."

June Hunt, Founder, Hope for the Heart
Author, *Caring for a Loved One with Cancer*

"An uplifting, spiritual journey that touches the soul; a reminder of God's unending love and devotion to all of us. Carmen Pate connects others to God in a personal, positive and friendly way, always leading by example. I recommend this book to all of my patients as well as friends and family."

Denise McShane,
RN, Oncology

"As my first mentor, Carmen Pate opened my eyes to what God could do with a broken young woman like I was. Now in this book, she opened my eyes again in how to journey through aggressive cancer—or other overwhelming battles that life throws at us—with joy instead of despair. Her determination to accept this trial as her 'next place to serve,' and bring glory to the God she loves, unfolds as an adventure of faith, hope and love that will inspire and empower every reader."

Kim Crabill, Founder,
Roses and Rainbows / Coffee, Inc.
Author, *Burdens to Blessings*

"Carmen Pate's beautiful book, *In Our Weakness, God is Strong,* will bring you to tears . . . of joy! Through deeply moving reflections and heartwarming excerpts from her hospital blog while battling Leukemia, Carmen shows us how suffering is an important part of our spiritual journey. Through Carmen's lived example, you'll see how God gives us the grace to face our own challenges, while divinely orchestrating opportunities to reveal Him to others in the midst of their suffering. Read this book, be inspired, and get ready to live an abundant, 'thank-you' life!"

David Bereit, Author, Speaker
Co-Founder, 40 Days for Life

"Carmen is a true inspiration! She has written a book that not only explores the trials and tribulations of what it's like to battle cancer, but also provides a very personal documentation of an amazing journey that proves the power of prayer is real. As a nurse, I recommend this book to anyone battling a life threatening disease. It is a brave chronicle that will inspire anyone on his or her own spiritual journey."

Katie Smith, RN, Oncology

"Life is more than escaping death. For the Christian, the purpose of life is not centered upon being happy. The purpose of life is to be holy, honorable, compassionate, in both good days as well as difficult days, and to be used by God for the glory of God. This is a life that makes a difference because it is a life well lived. This book shows you how to live well."

Fred Chay, Ph.D, Dean,
Doctorate of Ministry Program,
Grace School of Theology

"Del Fehsenfeld Jr., Founder of Life Action Ministries taught, 'to the degree that you can be open, honest and transparent about your sin - to that degree you can be free.' Carmen Pate is a living example of that truth. As you read this amazing book you will see how her life message has been developed through a lifetime of choices - both right and wrong. Carmen's openness, honesty and transparency have impacted my life. As her friend and former Pastor, I watched up close as she left behind success in the corporate world to serve in a variety of local nonprofit ministries. God placed her in significant national ministry assignments that have allowed her to impact many. Now her journey through physical pain and suffering has added another amazing chapter in her journey of faith. You will be challenged as you read Carmen Pate's life message. I couldn't put it down. As a chaplain, I know this is a resource that needs to be shared."

Dr. Forrest Lowry, Hospice Chaplain,
Baptist Pastor, Retired

"Such a needed book! Carmen magnificently weaves a tapestry of raw authenticity, the struggles of doubt and faith through desperate times, and especially the overcoming triumphs birthed out of an eternal perspective. A great read . . . and a great present for your friends."

Dwight Edwards, Best-Selling Author
Founder, Revolution Within Ministries

"Suffering causes many people to ask, 'Why me, Lord?' But, not Carmen Pate. On the darkest of days, she asks, 'What now, Lord?' because she knows there is no meaningless suffering for a child of God. Her inspiring story shows how we can experience God's power, presence, and peace in the midst of pain."

Kathy Peel, Journalist and Author of 22 books

IN OUR WEAKNESS, GOD IS STRONG

THE POWER OF HIS TOUCH THROUGH YOU

CARMEN PATE

To my grandchildren:
Sydney, Makayla, Quinneth, Sarah, Lyndon
Emily, Anson, and Molly
May you never fear the trials this life will bring.
God will use them to mature you,
and to draw you to a more
intimate relationship with Him, as you experience
His strength, faithfulness, and love.

CONTENTS

Acknowledgments xi

Foreword xiii

Introduction 1

Chapter 1: It's the Waiting 4

Chapter 2: The Adventure Begins 9

Chapter 3: Prayer Power 13

Chapter 4: I See Hurting People 17

Chapter 5: Superheroes 21

Chapter 6: Lifelines 25

Chapter 7: Do You Know Me? 31

Chapter 8: Why Me Lord? 35

Chapter 9: The Tough Days 39

Chapter 10: A Heart Softened 45

Chapter 11: Laughter, the Best Medicine 49

Chapter 12: The Veteran Among Us 53

Chapter 13: God's Golden Repair.................................... 60

Chapter 14: In My Weakness 65

Chapter 15: People Come and Go.................................. 70

Chapter 16: The New Normal...................................... 74

Chapter 17: Only By His Grace 78

Chapter 18: It's a Small World..................................... 82

Chapter 19: Lay Your Burdens Down 86

Chapter 20: Don't Lose Heart 91

Chapter 21: Just for a Season 96

Chapter 22: The Joy of the Lord................................... 100

Chapter 23: It's a God Thing 104

Chapter 24: Heart Imprints....................................... 108

Chapter 25: The Lost Sheep....................................... 113

Chapter 26: Wounded Hearts 117

Chapter 27: His Mysterious Ways 124

Chapter 28: Our Hope is in Christ................................. 129

Chapter 29: We Are Family.. 133

Chapter 30: God Still Performs Miracles 137

Chapter 31: The Thank-You Life 143

ACKNOWLEDGMENTS

After encouragement from family and friends to tell my story, the Lord's Spirit began to nudge me as well. I knew I could not write apart from His leading, and, with His help, the words flowed. So, I thank my Lord and Savior Jesus Christ for who I am in Him, and for His enabling power to do all things.

I am thankful for the young man in Europe, still unknown to me, who sacrificially donated his bone marrow so I might live to tell this story. And, to the many doctors, nurses, and PCA's at Houston Methodist Hospital who cared for me so well over a 3-year period through my illness and recovery. This book would not be possible without the stories of the patients and medical team. Though their names are changed to protect their privacy, the stories are shared out of my love for each one.

I am thankful every day for my husband, Bob, who has been my biggest cheerleader. He has prayed for me and encouraged me through my cancer journey and my writing. My dear friends Laurie Mott, Beryl Hartwig, Sheri Hunt, Christy and David Cahela have, together, reviewed, provided feedback, helped in editing, formatting and have simply been there for me, to do whatever was needed. I am most grateful for their tremendous help.

The staff of Grace School of Theology and Grace Theology Press has been behind me every step of the way to encourage, pray, and to counsel me through the process. A special thanks goes to Dr. Fred Chay, Joy Mendoza, Jana Lopena, Daniel Labry, Mark Rae, Ralene Berry and Tammie Jurek.

To all of my friends and family who financially gave to see the book published, thank you for sharing the journey through my battle with cancer and again through this journey to tell the story. I will be forever grateful for those friends who took time to write such wonderful endorsements.

And finally, I thank Dr. Dave Anderson, who kindly wrote the foreword, for helping me to grasp the love of Christ, a love that can never be earned, and can never be lost!

FOREWORD

When Carmen Pate first asked me to write an endorsement for her upcoming book, I was all too happy to do so. But when she finished the book, she said she had changed her mind about the endorsement. Instead she wanted me to write this foreword. I readily agreed but immediately felt waves of unworthiness flow over me. In this book, the curtains of heaven are peeled back, and we peek into a personal relationship with God that is so sacred and holy that I can almost visualize Carmen in the Holy of Holies like Isaiah with the angels shouting antiphonally back and forth, "Holy, holy, holy" (Isaiah 6:3). Only, in my imagination, it is not Isaiah in the temple witnessing this holy transaction. I am there, a man of unclean lips, thoroughly depraved. I fearfully look up, wondering if my eyes should gaze at this divine interaction between creature and Creator. I see the healing hand of God stretched out and resting on the brow of Carmen. The effulgent glory of God fills the temple as the angels once again shout, "Holy, holy, holy."

In her book on God's strength in the midst of our weaknesses, Carmen Pate captures for us not only the lessons God gave to her through her suffering with Acute Lymphoblastic Leukemia but also how God used her to strengthen others she met in the hospital. They had their own struggles with life, both physical and spiritual. She was truly a light in a dark tunnel of people suffering with cancer, marriage difficulties, career choices, financial struggles, and just life in general. She used her time in the hospital not to focus on herself as much as the struggles of others. If it weren't for her hair loss, you might have thought she was a hospital chaplain. Ultimately, her outreach touched not just other patients, but also hospital staff including nurses, and doctors.

Yet Carmen's story is not limited to her struggle with the strangling grip of death at the hospital. She reaches back into her days before she discovered the wonderful, freeing grace of Christ—the days before she fully experienced a love she did not have to earn and could never lose. She openly shares her deepest failures that drove her into deep despair—that dark night of the soul. But she also brings hope to all of us as she spells out how her Savior never gave up on her and had joys of splendor reserved for her she never could have imagined.

This, above all, is a book of hope—hope for anyone who has visited the bottomless pit of moral failure, disappointment with self, and the black hole of depression. But it is also a book of hope for those who have felt the ghastly grip of cancer or other terminal diseases. Carmen stared death in the face and came out alive. That obviously won't be true for all of us. But as we walk step by step with her, Carmen shows us how the most debilitating and discouraging days of our lives can also be the most fruitful. May this book be a hand God uses to lead you into green pastures, beside still waters, and, if need be, boldly through the valley of the shadow of death.

David R. Anderson, Ph.D.
President, Grace School of Theology

INTRODUCTION

And He said to me, "My grace is sufficient for you, for My strength is made perfect in weakness." Therefore most gladly I will rather boast in my infirmities, that the power of Christ may rest upon me.

2 Corinthians 12:9

The Abundant Life

"Hello, I'm Carmen Pate."

You may have heard this introduction many times on radio programs or podcasts that I have had the privilege of hosting. But you may not know that the distinctive southern voice that always sounds joyful on the air, is the same woman who personally knows about suffering. I want to invite you into that side of my world, to assure you that 'life breaks all of us,' as the novelist Ernest Hemingway, said.[1]

---

1 Ernest Hemingway, American journalist, novelist, 1899-1961.

My husband, Bob, and I are not new to the experience of trials in our lives. In fact, since we both discovered God's grace 20 years ago, and committed to serve God by sharing His grace with others, we have seen trials increase in intensity and endurance. We truly believe the enemy is not happy with our freedom in Christ, nor the joy and abundant life we now have. He certainly doesn't want us growing in grace, or sharing God's grace. In defiance of the enemy, our resolve to follow Christ more closely is stronger than ever.

So what about the trials? Are you saying, Carmen, that suffering is part of an abundant life? Absolutely! When we are confident of Christ's forgiveness of our sins and our eternal home with Him, no storm in life can sink our boat. Storms will rock our boat, but that boat will never sink!

Christ tells us things will get bad before He returns to make all things right, all things new. He says in John 16:33 (NLT) *I have told you all this so that you may have peace in Me. Here on earth you will have many trials and sorrows. But take heart, because I have overcome the world.*

I am so grateful for the truth found in God's Word that overpowers negative emotions during those times of trials and sorrow:

1. **God numbers our days.** A doctor's prognosis is only as good as medical science can determine. God has the last word.

2. **Christ always intercedes for us** for protection in our trials, and for strength through our suffering and sorrow, when we draw close to Him.

3. **Staying focused on God and His promises** gives us peace that surpasses human comprehension, even on the most difficult days.

4. **Worshiping and praising God in the midst of suffering** diminishes negative emotions and replaces them with joy.

5. **God's strength is magnified in our weakness** as we submit to His power in us.

6. **Our service to God during times of suffering** surprises those watching and brings opportunity for God to speak to them in a fresh way, allowing God to get all of the glory.

The abundant life? Yes! The power of God and intimacy with God, in the midst of trials and suffering, gives us strength in our weakness. The blessing of knowing God, deeper still, prompts many of us who have been through the valley to say, "Thank you Lord for this trial. I have never loved and trusted you more than I do now."

In this book, you will see me in my darkest moments. In excerpts from my daily hospital blog, written through the battle for my life—an aggressive relapse of Acute Lymphoblastic Leukemia, I pray you would also see the power of God working through my weakness to minister to those around me. Ernest Hemingway's complete quote reads: "Life breaks all of us, but many are made stronger in the broken places." That has been my experience, and my desire is that you, too, would be made stronger in the broken places. I will forever be amazed by His grace!

CHAPTER 1

IT'S THE WAITING

Be strong and courageous; don't be terrified or afraid.
For it is the Lord your God who goes with you; He will
not leave you or forsake you.

Deuteronomy 31:6 (paraphrase)

Anyone who has experienced cancer personally, or within his or her immediate family, knows that anticipating upcoming tests and scans, and waiting for the results, can be mentally and emotionally draining. It is the *not knowing* that causes you to wake up in the middle of the night and run through the myriad of *what ifs* running through your mind. It's not that you lose faith in God's control or His good purpose for your life, but you experience the disruption that cancer brings to your family routines and to future plans. You anticipate the pain, the sickness, and the recurring focus on dying that you can't seem to escape. Once you have a cancer diagnosis, your flesh doesn't want you to forget that it may return, even after years of remission.

My first diagnosis of cancer was in 2010—melanoma. Praise God, I was in remission from that particular cancer for over 8 years, and have only had a couple of melanoma spots removed since. But every three months when I go for a dermatologist appointment, that sense of restlessness returns. Particularly since, in 2015, I was diagnosed with another cancer—Chronic Myeloid Leukemia, which was found quite by accident. I say "accident," but the Lord orchestrated the discovery.

I rushed to the emergency room with a large, painful knot and bruise on my leg. I thought I had a blood clot. The wise ER doctor was more concerned about the multiple bruises he saw, and ordered blood work. Normal white blood count is within the 4000-10,000 range. Mine was over 140,000!

He sent me immediately for hospital admission, where I received the diagnosis. That was the beginning of my 3-year Leukemia journey. And, just as I do with scheduled dermatology check-ups, I turn to friends and family for prayer when appointments with my oncologist are scheduled:

May 16, 2018 (Morning)

Prayer warrior update: Dear friends and family, you have been so kind to pray for Bob and me, and we humbly ask for your continued prayers. My donor cell percentage dropped from 80 to 70, (normal is 100%) and abnormal cells in my blood have increased. I was scheduled to see my transplant doctor on May 29, but they asked me to come in today. So Bob and I are at Methodist Hospital, waiting. We are so grateful that God's plans for us are for His good purposes and, being confident of His never failing love, we wait in hopeful expectation! Thank you for praying as the Lord draws us to mind! We love you!

May 16 (Afternoon)

Bless you for your prayers and good wishes! I am so grateful for my transplant doctor and his team. They showed such compassion and took the necessary time needed to explain next steps. I will return on Friday for a bone marrow aspiration to help them determine exactly what they are dealing with. The doctor thinks perhaps my chemo has stopped working. They are switching to a daily chemo in hopes of getting me back in remission. There are other treatment options to consider, if I qualify. Additional tests must be done. My doctor told us he is presenting my unique case (my Leukemia changed from CML to ALL which is not the normal track; my donor cell percentage following the transplant never reached 100%) at a national Leukemia conference for transplant doctors. He is hopeful, as are we, that God will provide the answers. Feeling blessed beyond measure.

A measure of hope given by a trusted doctor during a time of waiting is a gift of strength from God in our weakness. The Lord always knows what we need to lift our spirits, to energize our bodies and minds, and to give us confidence in those He is working through on our behalf.

God also knows what the results of the tests will be, and regardless of the news, we can be confident that God will continue to work for us. His plan is always good and He is always faithful, so we can trust Him.

May 21, 2018

Thank you for continued prayers for Bob and me. My bone marrow aspiration on Thursday indicated a relapse. I will be admitted to the hospital tomorrow for a Chemo series over 4 days, followed by another bone marrow aspiration and lumbar puncture. Praying those tests will show remission once again. If so, I will get one last donor boost of cells. The doctor is working to get approval for a daily oral chemo that I will begin on my return home. God hasn't called me Home yet, so until then we will glorify His name through this journey! Thank you for joining us!

"For we do not have a High Priest who cannot sympathize with our weaknesses, but was in all points tempted as we are, yet without sin. Let us therefore come boldly to the throne of grace that we may obtain mercy and find grace, to help in time of need."

Hebrews 4:15-16

Bob and I wept hearing the word "relapse." We were both tired physically, mentally, emotionally. After my diagnosis with Chronic Myeloid Leukemia in July of 2015, the diagnosis changed August of 2016 to Acute Lymphoblastic

Leukemia and a bone marrow transplant was performed on February 28, 2017. We were approaching three years with cancer. Bob would often pull me close and say, "Sweet Pea, I know you are sick and tired of being sick and tired." And I was, but Bob was exhausted as well—spouses always are. However we knew, even as tears flowed, that this trial wasn't about either of us, but about God's purposes to receive glory in it. We could choose in those moments to move forward reluctantly with great despair; or to joyfully enter His great adventure for us, with the opportunity to know Him more intimately, and to allow God to touch others, through us. We both chose the latter!

CHAPTER TAKEAWAY: Many times in our lives we find ourselves waiting—for physical test results, for a check to come in, for a reply to a job application, for acceptance into college, etc. But when we are confident of God's love for us and His good purposes in our lives, we can have peace, regardless of the outcome.

PERSONAL REFLECTION: What are you waiting on? Are you trusting God with His perfect plan in your circumstances? Have you asked Him to give you His peace?

CHAPTER 2

THE ADVENTURE BEGINS

There's no higher dream than experiencing God as He moves through every circumstance of life to an eternal encounter with Himself where transformed people will enjoy perfectly loving community around Jesus Christ, the source of Perfect Love.[2]

Dr. Larry Crabb

Sometimes we don't know what God is doing in our circumstances but we can always trust that He is up to something bigger than our finite minds can understand.

Bob and I have moved several times in our marriage. Each time we both felt a leading from the Holy Spirit, and we were in agreement to move. But it wasn't always clear to

---

2 Dr. Larry Crabb, *Shattered Dreams: God's Unexpected Path to Joy* (2001).

us what God's purpose was in sending us to a new location. Each time it was truly a step of faith to go. And sometimes, only in looking back can we see, at least in part, God's purpose.

For those looking on, it might have appeared that our moves were for the sole purpose of a new job, or something connected to our work. God has certainly used our jobs to prompt a move. But Bob and I also knew that, wherever God sent us, it was about the people who needed to know His love and who needed to be loved by us—people who needed His touch through us. We often talk about the many great *God adventures* we have had, and our conversations revolve around the people whose lives impacted us, or whom we had the opportunity to impact for Christ.

One such move was to College Station, TX in 2007. Bob had his own business at the time and was working on a project with a Texas A&M scientist. That project was our purpose in moving there, or so we thought. Looking back, we would both tell you that the move was about our coffee shop ministry, which God had planned for us beforehand.

Bob and I took a coffee break each day at the local shop, where college students worked and hung out. We went there to read, sometimes with our Bibles, sometimes with non-fiction books written by various Christian authors. Employees or customers approached us regularly to ask questions or make comments about what we were reading. Those conversations led to friendships, which led to discipleship and mentoring opportunities.

Many Friday nights we opened our home for these students to bring music, poetry, or art to share. We would have a dozen or more students alternately entertaining, while Bob and I served homemade desserts and just loved on these kids. I started a Bible study in our home for the young ladies, and served a home-cooked meal as an incentive to come and bring a friend.

Bob met individually with young men struggling with various issues, leading some to Christ and others to a more intimate fellowship with the Lord. We invited the students to study in our home and to consider us as extended family.

We stay in touch with many of them to this day, and thank God for the lives we saw Him transform by His grace. Those two years in College Station provide some of our fondest ministry memories. But you don't have to move to a new location to have a great adventure with God. Sometimes it happens in a hospital setting.

May 22, 2018

Thank you Lord for this day of blessings! Upon arrival at the hospital, the registrar asked about my transplant experience. She has been given opportunity to have a stem cell transplant for her own diagnosis, but is hesitant and quite anxious. We had a good discussion about God's love for us and His perfect plan for our lives. I told her how He had given her the opportunity to work here so she might learn more about her disease, and also to have access to an incredible medical team. I asked if God had ever been unfaithful to her, knowing she would say "never." I asked if I might pray for her and she said "yes," so I did. Another employee came in as we were praying and joined us. We had a group hug after the "Amen." In those few moments God reminded me that this is not about me, but the many all around who are hurting and broken, and need to know the love of Jesus! That would be all of us, right?

> After a full day that included insertion of a picc line, blood work (22 vials), x-ray, and echo, I am ready for Chemo. I have tentatively qualified for the CarT cell clinical trials (T cells are collected, modified into CarT cells and infused back into body) and, I was approved for the new oral chemo! Not bad for day one! Thank you Lord, and thanks to each of you for covering me in your prayers!

CHAPTER TAKEAWAY: Walking with God is the greatest adventure we can experience in this life. When we love Him and desire to show others who He is through our love, the opportunities He will give us are unlimited.

PERSONAL REFLECTION: Have you thought of your life as an adventure with God to show the world who He really is? Have you asked God to grow your love for Him through your trials so that His love overflows through you?

CHAPTER 3

PRAYER POWER

Be anxious for nothing, but in everything by prayer and supplication, with thanksgiving, let your requests be made known to God; and the peace of God, which surpasses all understanding, will guard your hearts and minds through Christ Jesus.

Philippians 4:6-7

The power of prayer is undeniable. I'll never forget my first experience of God directly answering a prayer for a hospital procedure, back in 2010. I arrived at a Dallas hospital for 7:00 AM surgery to remove a melanoma from between my shoulder blades. A dear friend of ours, Dr. Sumner Wemp, a retired seminary professor from Liberty University, and an incredible prayer warrior, was there to pray with Bob and me. Also with us was Dr. Steve Nutter, a gentle man with a shepherd's heart, and the pastor of our church at that time, Community Bible Church of Irving, TX. Bob and I were incredibly humbled and blessed by the presence of these godly men who loved us, and whom we loved. "Dr. Wemp, I am so grateful that you came," I said. "The Lord nudged me to come," he replied. Upon Dr. Nutter's arrival, Bob welcomed him and he replied, "I wouldn't be anywhere else. God made it clear I was to be here to pray for you both." Bob and I were confident God would hear their prayers, and ours.

I had delayed seeing a dermatologist far too long, and the cancer was large and deep. The oncologist warned me that the most painful part of this surgery experience would be the multiple shots he would inject around this very sensitive location, necessary for deadening the area. Having not experienced this now common procedure, I was terrified! My specific prayer request to Bob, Dr. Wemp and Dr. Nutter was that God would not allow the shots to be painful. I remember well, lying on the hard table in that sterile operating room, the kind oncologist saying, "I am so sorry, but this is going to hurt. Hold your breath." But it didn't hurt! Nor did the other nine shots he gave me in that "very sensitive" area. I knew God had answered our prayers! "Praise the Lord! No pain," I shouted. The surprised doctor and nurse attending simply smiled in agreement. It was truly a faith builder for me, and hopefully for them. God knew I would need faith in the power of prayer for the difficult years to come.

MAY 23, 2018

I wish I could explain how I "feel" your prayers! God is hearing and He is at work on my behalf. The first three Chemo doses were given through the night. This is aggressive chemo, but today I have had no side effects.

In fact, I have an appetite, I have walked, and felt strong enough to encourage others!

As I was walking, I saw a patient in her room weeping. I learned that this sister in Christ had experienced one setback after another. I could certainly empathize, and I told her that I cry, too. Cancer is a terrible disease. But I also told her I am learning to take my focus off the cancer and to focus instead on my identity in Christ and all of the benefits we have as believers. Our situation is truly a win-win for us. Should the Lord take us Home, we will be with our Savior and loved ones who have gone before us. We will be completely healed, never to be sick again! If God should heal us here, then He has a purpose for us yet to fulfill, and we have the opportunity to continue loving our loved ones on earth, with His love. She said she wanted to change her focus and we prayed that she would be able!

Tonight, throughout the night, I receive my second series of three Chemo treatments. The doctor told me I would be in the hospital at least a month. Please pray particularly against bad side effects that can happen beginning the 3rd week. By then I will lose my hair a second time, due to Chemo! The adventure continues and I praise Him for the peace and joy He is giving me through it all. Thank you for joining me, on what has turned out to be a very long journey!

CHAPTER TAKEAWAY: Prayer is the greatest tool we have to communicate our needs to the Lord who loves us. God hears the prayers of His people,

and He is pleased when we trust He will answer according to what is best for us.

PERSONAL REFLECTION: Have you reflected on the many prayers God has answered in your own journey? Is He prompting you to talk with Him more often, or to ask others to pray for you?

CHAPTER 4

I SEE HURTING PEOPLE

Your Father knows your gifts, your hindrances, and the condition you're in at every moment. And He also knows something you can't possibly know—every single person who's in desperate need of receiving His touch through you.[3]

Bruce H. Wilkinson

If you are looking for a person to pray with, someone who truly has a hunger and need for somebody to pray for them, or with them, you will find abundant opportunities in a hospital. Over the years, I have visited friends or family in the hospital to encourage and pray with them but, I focused solely on the person I came to see, someone I knew and who knew me. My eyes were not open

---

3 Bruce Wilkinson, *The Prayer of Jabez: Breaking Through to the Blessed Life* (2000).

to the need that existed all around me. Hurting people fill every room in a hospital—those who are sick, worried love ones, the medical team of individuals who each have their own trials, but are committed and focused on the care of their patients, and not their own concerns.

The Lord graciously opened my eyes as a patient to the fear, doubt, pain and uncertainty of those around me. Focusing on others helped to take my focus off my own fear, doubt, pain and uncertainty. For those moments when I focused on those around me, I experienced courage, energy and passion that could only be described as supernatural. I felt unexplainable joy that could only be the Holy Spirit loving on others through me. God proved, once again, that His power is made perfect in my weakness.

May 24, 2018

Grateful for another day of God's sufficient grace! I woke feeling refreshed after a second full night of 3 rounds of chemo! No nausea! So I took my first walk around 6:00 AM. I have my "track" laid out all around my floor, which includes the waiting area for the transplant center. Seeing two women waiting for the 8:00 AM opening, I knew they must have come to the hospital early to avoid Houston rush hour traffic. I spoke and then circled back, asking who was the patient. The elder of the two said she was there for blood transfusions. Her daughter brings her each week and holds her hand. I smiled to think of the love her daughter surely had for her precious mom. I asked if I could pray for them both and they were eager for me to do so! They both were thanking Jesus aloud as I prayed, and I knew He was in this place.

In a later walk, another patient was coming out of her room, so she joined me. This precious woman from Lebanon escaped the country years ago, with her family, during a time of persecution there. She has Leukemia and is in line for a bone marrow transplant. She asked that I pray for her 14 year old daughter who is not handling well the fact of her mom being so sick. Her grades are dropping and she has become depressed. I directed her to the wonderful support groups offered for families, as well as the wonderful Chaplain team here at the hospital. After we prayed she was off to check out those resources.

A precious young grandma was crying in the waiting room. I sat down and asked if she had a loved one here. Her teenage grandson has been here for 2 months and is not doing well. We cried together as I could not imagine the pain if my grandchild were going through this. I asked if I might pray for her and for her grandson and family. She was so thankful. We prayed and cried some more to a loving God who loves our grandkids, even more than we do.

Another sweet patient commented on my silver hair, as she ran her fingers through her own long, thinning hair, to show me it was falling out. I told her she was beautiful, and she cried. I asked God to let her see herself, as He sees her. Later when I was walking by her room she was doing her nails! Sometimes it is the little things that make us feel like the princesses we are!

> As for me, I get the next set of Chemo tonight. Please pray God continues to give me the strength and endurance needed for another day! Much love and eternal thanks!

CHAPTER TAKEAWAY: God places people all around us who are hurting and broken. He desires we recall the compassion He has shown us so we might show others that same compassion. Focusing on others, instead of our own pain, brings peace and joy to our circumstances and theirs.

PERSONAL REFLECTION: Have you asked God to open your eyes to the needs of those around you? Are you trusting God to give you His strength and guidance to be of help, to pray, or to simply encourage someone?

CHAPTER 5

SUPERHEROES

If you pour yourself out for the hungry and satisfy the desire of the afflicted, then shall your light rise in the darkness and your gloom be as the noonday. And the Lord will guide you continually and satisfy your desire in scorched places and make your bones strong; and you shall be like a watered garden, like a spring of water, whose waters do not fail.

Isaiah 58:10-11 (ESV)

If you spend much time in the hospital as a patient, you learn quickly who the heroes really are. The medical teams of doctors, nurses and patient care assistants (PCAs)in Houston's Methodist Hospital oncology and transplant wing make the patient a top priority. My admiration and respect have grown immensely for their dedication, knowledge, skill and professionalism. They possess an incredible ability to joyfully serve, in spite of difficult patients and life-or-death circumstances. Many often forget that they have a life outside of the hospital and they, too, experience personal trials in life. No doubt, they are also waiting to receive God's touch through someone who cares.

May 25, 2018

My prayer encounters with the incredible nurses here is such a privilege, as they each work tirelessly, extremely long hours, and nurture and care for us as though we are the only ones who suffer. But you learn that they, too, have trials when you take time to listen—Like the nurse who comes in the room singing joyfully. I call her "SONshine." She shared how her nuclear family is blessed, but her extended family suffers with serious issues that impact her family. They don't share her faith and her heart breaks for them. But, she daily leaves those troubles behind, in order to bring sunshine to our day.

And another nurse, who lives with constant pain after numerous surgeries, yet works 12-hour shifts, walking up and down these halls. I never heard her complain, but I asked how I might pray for her, and she shared her trial.

And finally, my kindred spirit night nurse who took care of me the very first night I was admitted for Chemo in 2016. We learned then that our pasts were so similar— corporate life, failures in life, and our amazing stories of God's grace and mercy! She is a brilliant woman, and found her ministry calling in loving, nurturing and helping to heal oncology patients! Yet she too, has personal trials and sorrows. What a joy to pray for these nurses and to be inspired by their dedication to "the least of these." Amazed by His grace!

May 26, 2018

I was blessed to have another good day following my last round of intensive chemo. The oral chemo I have now started seems to be working well. A few side effects appeared today including intense muscle cramps and nausea, but nothing of concern to the medical team. So I knew the Lord was going to let me make my rounds another day. I continued to focus on the doctors and nurses today. They are all exhausted. One MD, I would guess in his mid-thirties, who has a tremendous bedside manner, told me this was his 8th, twelve-hour day in a row, with four more to go. His wife is a Resident in another building, and they have a two year old! "We are trying to figure out how to slow down before our little girl grows up," he said. He became teary eyed as he spoke of his daughter's newest words. I asked if I could pray. He lit up and said, "Yes, please do." He said he appreciated me asking, and for praying for His strength, endurance and discernment with his family's priorities.

A PCA, who was caring for me, came in when I was reading the Bible. "I could use your prayers," she said as she wrapped the blood pressure cuff around my arm. "My daughter is in her early teens and thinks she is 21," she continued. Anyone who has had teens can relate to her dilemma! The PCA's long, but necessary, work hours keep her from being with her daughter as she desires, and she fears for her choices while away. I prayed for her and we explored some ideas she hopes to pursue.

My sweet nurse that I call "Hannah" desires a child with her whole being. When I was in the hospital before, I told her the story of Hannah (1 Samuel 1). We prayed that she would release her burden to the Lord, and have faith that He would allow what is best for her and her husband. Her update was that she had lost a child since I was last in, and they are now prayerfully considering adoption. I cried with her over her loss and encouraged her in praying to adopt. I also gave her resource numbers should she want to explore adoption further.

I was reminded today that though there is much death and dying that happens here, God desires to give us all opportunity for real, abundant life, every day. He says, "Come to me, all you who are weary and burdened, and I will give you rest. Take my yoke upon you and learn from me, for I am gentle and humble in heart, and you will find rest for your souls. For my yoke is easy and my burden is light." (Matthew 11:28-30 NIV) I pray these tireless servants find that rest and abundant life in Christ.

CHAPTER TAKEAWAY: Medical teams of doctors, nurses and PCA's are selfless servants. The best are those who feel called to care for others. Their passion and hard work are poured out daily. They deserve our recognition and prayers.

PERSONAL REFLECTION: Have you noticed the tremendous care you or a loved one has received from the medical team? Have you considered ways you might show your appreciation?

CHAPTER 6

LIFELINES

Two are better than one, because they have a good reward for their labor. For if they fall, one will lift up his companion, but woe to him who is alone when he falls, for he has no one to help him up.

Ecclesiastes 4:9-10

od created us to desire and experience community with one another, just as the Trinity—Father, Son and Holy Spirit—enjoy community. In the garden before Eve was created, God said of Adam, *It is not good that man should be alone; I will make him a helper comparable to him.* (Genesis 2:18) We humans need one another, especially through our trials. But often, in our pride and self-sufficiency, we think we can do life on our own. We don't want to admit we need help, and might tend to reject help that is offered. I recognized this was a weak area in my life that God wanted to correct.

As a cancer patient, and then a transplant patient, there were times I could not drive, shop, clean house, cook, or do other normal activities. I would often break down in tears because I had always been so independent. Since Bob often travels with his job, I had to ask friends and family for help on many occasions, and it was very difficult for me to do so. I felt like a different person, and I didn't like the new me.

Sometimes, my prideful independence had to be confronted when I tried to do things on my own, or in ways that would be harmful to me. I would try to carry groceries that were now too heavy for me to carry, or try to do housework or exercise beyond what I knew were my limits. But the kindness shown and sacrificial help given, by my husband and other family and friends, though humbling, have been a tremendous blessing. Our daughter cleaned our apartment. Friends ran errands and drove me to doctor appointments and treatments. It has taught me to see the joy in both giving and receiving. I learned that God often strengthens our weaknesses through others.

May 27, 2018

Thanking God for a restful day and time to be filled spiritually, so I might be better prepared to pour out. I had more intense time in the Word and in prayer. I am so blessed by the many who pour into me through music and teaching online, and by the chaplains who come by and pray with me and offer communion. But I am most grateful today for my precious husband, Bob, my spiritual mentor and best friend. He studies and prays with me. We talk about the near future and eternity, with joy and with tears. Bob loves the Lord with all of his heart, and as a result he loves me as Christ commands and is the perfect man for me through good times and bad.

His work ethics are impeccable and he will not miss work, ever. We are so grateful for the Lord's provision of income and benefits through his work, and he wants to serve his company well to honor our Lord. Last year, when I was in the hospital months at a time, Bob would literally make two, 3 hour round trips, each day to come see me before and after work. Then he would go home to take care of all the things I normally would have done. I could see he was quickly going downhill from extreme exhaustion and stress.

So we made a pact this time around. He will only visit on weekends (unless an emergency arises), when he can avoid the heaviest of Houston traffic and not be stressed by the workday, to spend time with me. On his work days, we text or call throughout the day, and end the evening with a phone call and prayer.

Often people forget that the spouse goes through cancer too—mentally, emotionally, and the physical stress of keeping up can be overwhelming. I am so grateful for a husband who also finds his strength in the Lord, and I so appreciate all of you who are praying for him, and for other caretakers around the world. They, too, are heroes!

As for me, my fourth day of chemo is behind me. The last of the series is tonight. God has heard your prayers and continues to spare me the awful side effects. I have 30–40 more days in the hospital while my system hits rock bottom and then builds back up, hopefully, in preparation for the clinical trial CarT cells as a possible cure. Thanking God for each of you who pour into my life daily through prayers, scriptures and encouraging words! I am most blessed!

May 28, 2018

"Be still," are hard words for me to hear. My type "A" temperament and OCD habits will drive anyone crazy who has to live with me. Bob has said all through our marriage, "You never sit and just rest." I always keep pushing, pushing, particularly to meet my workout goals regardless, and often, to my detriment.

When I entered the hospital in 2016, a dear friend confronted me about this compulsion (iron sharpens iron), and asked me to think spiritually about what I was trying to do. I knew what she meant. Beyond the healthy goals of taking care of my body, my flesh thought if I could just walk more often, and at a faster pace, I could steer the cancer away. I thought trying harder might heal me. My friend challenged me: "Perhaps the Lord is allowing this season for a time of rest—rest for your body and rest for your mind, away from the trap of performance." Wise words. I heeded them well for a short season, but found myself once again trying to walk off my cancer when I relapsed.

But last night was a breakthrough for me. My night nurse asked if she could make an observation and I said, "Yes., of course!" She continued, "You know, I watch you walk the halls like you are in a speed race. It scares me for you, because you will need that extra energy when your body crashes, and you won't have it. " I thanked her, told her to slow me down in the halls, and committed to cut back on time walking.

After she left the room, I asked the Lord to reveal my heart. " What is really going on Lord? " I immediately saw my pride in trying to control my destiny, focusing on the temporary instead of the eternal and, frankly, my denial of the cancer. I confessed my pride, and God always forgives. I was reminded of 1 Timothy 4:7b-8: " Exercise yourself toward godliness. For bodily exercise profits a little, but godliness is profitable for all things, having promise of the life that now is and of that which is to come. " May I learn this lesson well and be still, knowing He is indeed God.

As for my health, counts are all dropping as expected. We are hoping we can begin the CarT cell trial over the next couple of days, while the cancer cells are still there, so they may be destroyed! Please pray to that end, and also that my heart and lungs will hold up through the process. I'm so thankful for each of your prayers and love!

CHAPTER TAKEAWAY: We often think we don't need help, that we can handle life's trials on our own. Sometimes our pride leads us to refuse help that is offered. But God created us to serve one another. Life is easier and blessed when we give and receive help.

PERSONAL REFLECTION: Are you allowing others to use their gifts and talents to minister to you in your time of need? Do you see the blessing others receive in serving you?

CHAPTER 7

DO YOU KNOW ME?

The Goal of our spiritual influence on others is to cooperate with God in helping them fulfill their whole potential in Christ. It's to be used by God to help others become more like Jesus.[4]

Dwight Edwards

We may think we know a person because we've met them. The person may live next door and we know they have a family, because we see them together in the yard and see them coming and going together. We say they are nice people because they greet us and have never been rude. We may say they are Christian because perhaps we see them leave home on Sundays with Bibles in their hands. But do we really know them? Have we

---

4 Dwight Edwards, *Releasing the Rivers Within: The Exhilaration of Utter Dependence on God* (2003), 53.

taken time to invest in their lives by getting to know them at a deeper level?

Paul the Apostle wanted to "know" Christ, the power of His resurrection, the fellowship of His sufferings. Paul was a believer in Jesus Christ as the Messiah, his Redeemer, but he wanted to know Christ on a deeper level, because He wanted to conform to Christ's life. To know Christ intimately can only be accomplished by spending more time with Him, in His Word and in prayer. To really know those He loves, and to hopefully shine Christ's light into their darkness, requires us spending time with people and hearing, not only their stories, but also their hearts.

I have not yet arrived in learning to really hear what others are saying but, as I practice doing so, the Holy Spirit teaches me how to pray for that person. I get to experience God working through me to touch others where they need Him most.

May 29, 2018

There is always more to the story...my new, fellow-patient friend, Tina, whom I had understood to say that her family fled persecution in Lebanon in the 70's, clarified over the last couple of days that her family came to USA for business during that time period. She was raised Muslim, but is not devout. She said her husband has no faith, but she believes in a higher power. Since she doesn't know to whom to pray, she prays to Allah. Someone gave her a Bible, so she also prays to Jesus. "Anyone up there who will listen," she said. I told her that I just happen to have a personal relationship with Jesus, and would be happy to introduce her to my

Savior. I shared the simple gospel message, and she said that she really needed to learn more, and asked if I could help. I am so excited for the opportunity to share with Tina the hope and joy that I have in Jesus through these difficult days. I have ordered a book for her: Seeking Allah, Finding Jesus by Nabeel Qureshi5, in hopes of continuing our dialogue. Pray the Holy Spirit will guide our conversations!

And, there is more to Miss Maria's story, too. She is the sweet lady who cried over her hair loss. It took a couple of days before I learned that this older patient, in addition to Leukemia, also has Dementia! I don't know if we can understand the difficulty of this added illness for the family, the medical team and for the patient. She has to be monitored closely as she tries to leave with purse in hand to go shopping, and as typical with Dementia patients, she is very confused about her circumstances. But she is also a joy! She tells everyone that she and I have known each other for 40 years and that we both got cancer in Greece when we were kids. She told her son that I was her best friend. So, I try to check in on her regularly throughout the day, and tell her that God and I love her. Pray for the medical team and for her family to discern what is best for her needs. I better rest up as Miss Marie may come get me to "go shopping."

My counts continue to drop and I get weaker each day—no alarm I am told, just the process, but I sense

---

5 Nabeel Qureshi, *Seeking Allah, Finding Jesus: A Devout Muslim Encounters Christianity* (2014). Nabeel died from stomach cancer in 2017, at the age of 34.

anxiety arising in my spirit. I will take it to the Lord. Love and thanks to each of you for continued prayers! Amazed by His grace!

CHAPTER TAKEAWAY: To know God at a deeper level requires time with Him in His word and in prayer. Getting to know others with a desire to help, or to influence them with the truth of God's love, requires an investment of time into their lives.

PERSONAL REFLECTION: Do you desire to know God more intimately? Are there people you have wanted to know on a deeper level? Ask God to help you be more intentional about spending time with Him and with others.

CHAPTER 8

WHY ME LORD?

A touch comes, and you know it is the right hand of God. It is not the hand of restraint, or discipline, but of inexpressible peace, comfort, and the sense that underneath, are the everlasting Arms, full of support, provision, comfort, and strength.[6]

Oswald Chambers

A diagnosis of cancer brings with it questions. Among them, "Why me?" "Am I being punished?"

Cancer is not God's punishment. Jesus Christ paid our punishment for sin, in full, when He died on the cross. The fact is we live in a cursed, fallen world. Bad things happen. But God only allows His children to suffer what has been filtered through His loving hands. In other words, He

---

6   Oswald Chambers, *My Utmost for His Highest* (Dodd & Mead Publishers, 1935).

will only allow what can be used for His good purposes in our lives.

Walking closely with God (seeking God daily through time in His word and prayer) does not eliminate suffering, but provides the greatest way to endure it. As we trust His plan and find contentment in Him in each moment of our trial, His Holy Spirit matures us and transforms us to be more like Christ in the process. We become witnesses of His glory.

God is gracious and merciful and knows the limits of our weak, finite bodies. In His grace, if we believe in Christ as our Savior, He may allow some of His children to end their battle with cancer and go Home to Him where we will be made perfectly whole and suffer no more. He may choose to carry others through the battle of cancer and give them more days on this earth. Either case is victory for the believer!

God is always good, loving and perfect in His ways. His desire in all circumstances is to draw people to Himself. Each of us are made right with God when we trust Christ for forgiveness of sins. At that moment, death no longer has a hold over us! To be absent from the body is to be present with the Lord! God will right all wrongs when Christ returns, and removes the curse that now exists in creation. Come Lord Jesus!

May 30, 2018

Approaching my 3rd year in this battle with Leukemia, I had chosen to forget the 2015 onset and the "turn your world upside down" news I received then. The Lord reminded me today because Betsy and her family are facing this afresh, and needed encouragement and prayer from someone who could empathize. Her daughter and her husband approached me and asked about my "positive attitude." I briefly commented that I know God loves me; He has a purpose in this disease for my good, and for His purposes; and I can trust God with His plan. As a believer I have nothing to fear and, regardless of the outcome, I win. They said they were Christians and believe as I do but right now Betsy is overwhelmed with the news and fear of the unknown. Betsy is still reeling from the punch.

I remembered being where Betsy is now. It was not spiritual platitudes, which I fear is what I gave them, that gave me peace then, or now. I had the same fears, doubts and questions that, no doubt, Betsy has. I struggled with the "Why me?" and "Is God punishing me?" questions. I sought answers in the Bible and in prayers. I asked spiritual mentors for insight. And God, in His grace, reminded me at that time of who He is, of His power, His presence, His faithfulness and His love. Over time, peace that passes understanding filled my heart and mind and, thankfully, has stayed with me. I plan to visit Betsy tomorrow and I pray the Lord will allow me to bring His peace to her circumstances. I love the quote, "Job never knew why he suffered, but He saw God, and that was enough." I pray Betsy discovers God is enough!

I am still in the "crash" mode with my blood counts. I was declared "neutropenic" today, which basically means I am more prone to possible infections, and so extra measures are being taken to protect me. I am still in line for CarT cells. Prayers please for continued strength and protection of my organs. Love and thanks eternally.

CHAPTER TAKEAWAY: God's eternal perspective on our circumstances is always one of peace and hope because of what Christ has done for us through the cross. When we have trusted Jesus for forgiveness of sins, we become part of God's family, and we have the blessing of eternal life with Him.

PERSONAL REFLECTION: Have you trusted Christ's finished work on the cross to cover your sins past, present, and future? Do you have peace that you will spend eternity with Jesus? Do you know that by faith alone, you can be sure?

CHAPTER 9

THE TOUGH DAYS

Therefore we do not lose heart. Even though our outward man is perishing, yet the inward man is being renewed day by day. For our light affliction, which is but for a moment, is working for us a far more exceeding and eternal weight of glory, while we do not look at the things which are seen, but at the things which are not seen. For the things which are seen are temporary, but the things which are unseen are eternal.

2 Corinthians 4:16-18

Facing your mortality is a humbling experience, but in my journey, I finally really understood what I professed to know all along—that God is truly in control of my destiny. The stages of grief I had only read about actually unfolded, as described, in dealing with my own cancer diagnosis and prognosis:

- Denial/Isolation;

- Anger/Resentment;

- Bargaining/Works;
- Depression/Alienation.

But God doesn't leave us in grief. In the book, *God's Healing for Life's Losses*,[7] the stages of healing are described and, by His grace, those have been my experience as well:

- Waiting/Trusting with Faith;
- Wailing/Groaning with Hope;
- Weaving/Perceiving with Grace;
- Worshipping/Engaging with Love.

God is doing a work in me, and He desires I let Him.

The Christian artists, *Casting Crowns,* released a song, early on in my diagnosis, that has so encouraged me. The title is "Just Be Held." It says, in part:

Hold it all together
Everybody needs you strong
life hits you out of nowhere
And barely leaves you holding on

And when you're tired of fighting
Chained by your control
There's freedom in surrender
Lay it down and let it go

So when you're on your knees
And answers seem so far away

---

7   Robert W. Kellemen, *God's Healing for Life's Losses: How to Find Hope When You're Hurting* (BMH Books, 2010).

You're not alone, stop holding on
And just be held.[8]

These words described my feeling exactly during those days. I was tired of fighting, but God continued to remind me that the battle was His, and He would daily encourage me to rest in Him and not give up. I am so thankful for the encouragement and worship experience that comes through music and books. But I am most thankful for personal encounters, people I meet on my rounds or friends who visit, in which I receive God's touch of love through others, at just the right time.

During particularly rough days when I was feeling very weak, very sick, alone and sad, God showed up through friends who visited and through opportunities for me to serve others. He always knows what we need!

May 31, 2018

The Lord knew that I needed to be ministered to today. My weakest day, thus far, I have stayed fairly close to, or in, my room. Two dear friends came by, separately, to encourage and to pray with me. Neither friend required conversation, but just wanted to be with me. One brought much-needed boxes of SOFT tissues, (a huge blessing as a continual runny nose has caused the area to be raw and tender). The other treated me to a refreshing green iced tea. They both left books to feed my soul. I am so thankful for these friends, and I am so thankful for

---

8   "Just Be Held," by Casting Crowns, Released 2014.

each of you for lifting me up daily, as though you were here with me.

God gives each one gifts to minister to others, and no matter how great or small, ministry done in love is like a warm blanket that surrounds people with God's love. I am feeling your love and I am blessed. Prayers for strength are needed, please. Thank you!

June 1, 2018 (Morning)

After a very difficult night with high fever and chills, I am praising God this morning for bringing me through it all. This passage expresses my heart: "I love the Lord, because He has heard my voice and my supplications. Because He has inclined His ear to me, therefore I will call upon Him as long as I live. The pains of death surrounded me . . . I found trouble and sorrow. Then I called upon the name of the Lord: 'O Lord, I implore You, deliver my soul!' Gracious is the Lord, and righteous; yes, our God is merciful. The Lord preserves the simple; I was brought low, and He saved me. Return to your rest, O my soul, for the Lord has dealt bountifully with you." Psalm 116:1–7

June 1 (Evening)

Stay in your room and they will come! Because of my high fever last night, and being in a neutropenic state, I was isolated in my room today. But what a glorious day it was! It started with the morning PCA who asked if I would pray for her regarding her continuing education. She wants to be an RN, following her dad's footsteps. He had been her cheerleader to pursue her dream, and then he passed. She said she lost her drive and motivation after that, yet deep inside she knows that is her calling. We had a wonderful talk about purpose and calling and how your greatest joy comes when your passions and gifts fall in line with what you do! I encouraged her to go through The 210 Project, an online assessment and discovery tool that has helped thousands discover their calling. We prayed for her to have the courage to move forward, the wisdom to learn and retain, the motivation to study hard and let God deliver the results! Pray for Jeanne.

My day nurse is one who cared for me so well during 2016. She became one of my "adopted" spiritual daughters and we have stayed in touch. It was such a blessing to pour into her life today and to hear of her own journey this past year. I believe God is working in her life, and in her boyfriend's life, and I pray they will be sensitive to His leading. Pray for Kathy.

I was pleasantly surprised to have a visit by a male nurse, from the Bone Marrow Transplant side of the wing. This small stature, Asian man took such good care of me there during my months in that unit. I called him my "silent angel," as he was not only quiet spoken, but also a man of very few words. I would ask, "How can I pray for you today?" He would grin and say, "That my daughter would marry." He came into the room today and said, "My daughter married!" So now we are praying for grandchildren!

As evening approaches my fever is beginning to spike, and I am lying here packed in ice. I am also dealing with infection today, so I am connected to IV antibiotics. But I am peacefully resting in the fruit that God allowed me to bear today. I know I will rest well. Bless you for continued prayers!

CHAPTER TAKEAWAY: Our trials and times of suffering and loss can bring on many stages of grief, but God doesn't leave us there. He uses people and circumstances to encourage us through words, music, acts of kindness and more.

PERSONAL REFLECTION: In times of grief, do you look for ways to take your focus off your sorrow? Have you considered the joy of music, or reading the Psalms, or visiting with a loved one or friend?

CHAPTER 10

A HEART SOFTENED

Search me, O God, and know my heart; try me, and know my anxieties; and see if there is any wicked way in me, and lead me in the way everlasting.

Psalm 139:23-24

None of us are immune to bitterness when we harbor an unforgiving spirit. Personally, I learned this lesson years ago, when I felt betrayed by someone I deeply admire. We had worked closely together, and I believed my intentions toward her were always good. I looked forward to working alongside her for many years but, overnight, our friendship ended. She took personally what I thought was constructive criticism for the organization we represented. Hurtful words that I felt were aimed toward my character, wounded my heart and we parted ways. I wasn't just hurt—I was angry! Because of my pride, I could not accept the possibility that I might have hurt her. I believed I was the only victim.

After months of anger, which turned to bitterness, I found myself *placed on a shelf* by the Lord. It seemed that both work and ministry opportunities stopped. One morning, while listening to a sermon on tape, I was convicted of my sin of pride and bitterness. But what surprised me was that the Lord was telling me to ask her for forgiveness!

"But Lord, what did I do?" God made it clear that, even if I felt I had done nothing wrong, my friend was obviously hurt by my actions. That fact alone made my actions towards her wrong.

So, I wrote a letter to my friend and asked her to forgive me. I also committed to the Lord to forgive her for the hurt she caused me, and to pray for her every single day, which I do to this day. I can say sincerely that I overcame my bitterness long ago, and I feel nothing but love for her.

June Hunt, Founder and CSO of *Hope for the Heart* said, "Forgiveness is releasing your resentment toward your offender. Releasing your right to hear, 'I'm sorry.'"[9] God softened my heart and restored my ministry, once I obeyed the Spirit and let go of my resentment. And now, it appeared God desired to soften another bitter heart, but this time, through me.

June 2, 2018

There's one in every crowd...the naysayer. You perhaps have known such a person— always negative, always complaining, always raining on everyone else's parade. I

---

9 June Hunt, "Forgiveness, Quick Reference Counseling Keys Excerpt," adapted from Hope for the Heart's Biblical Counseling Library.

met Donna at the coffee bar in our wing, after my first week here. After introducing myself and asking how she was doing, she began reviewing a long list of why this place was the "next closest thing to hell." I told her I was sad to hear of her misery and asked if I might pray with her. She responded, "OK, but it won't do any good." I prayed that she would have eyes to see the good around her and grow to be thankful for the tremendous care she receives. Before parting, I told her perhaps we could talk again on a better day.

This morning, Donna approached me and said, "I need to talk to you." So we stepped aside in the hallway, and she said, "They (medical staff) don't like me, but I can see they like you, why is that?"

I assured her that they love her, and are committed to her healing. I said, "Perhaps the difference might be that they know that I love them."

"How do they know that?" she asked.

So I told her that every morning I ask the Lord to help me be a blessing to all those around me, and never a burden due to a negative attitude. I am conscious of that prayer as I go about the day, and look for opportunities to love on people.

She replied, "Well I don't want to be a burden." She hesitated and said, "So I guess we are going to pray about it?"

I laughed and told her that was a good place to start. When we parted, she called back "God bless you!"

I look forward to getting to know Donna better, and to tell her more about my Jesus, the One who lives in and through me to love others. Pray for my new friend.

As for me, I had a full body CT scan today. Results just came in, and the spread of cancer to my organs was not evident. Praises! I do have a blood infection they are working tirelessly to resolve, as the infection causes dangerously high fevers. I am confident they will. God is hearing your prayers dear friends and family! I don't take even one of those prayers for granted. May you all be blessed!

CHAPTER TAKEAWAY: Bitterness and unforgiveness will destroy any chance of experiencing God's peace and joy in our life. God is faithful to forgive when we confess our sin. He will then empower us to forgive those who have hurt us.

PERSONAL REFLECTION: Are there people whom you believe have hurt you, that you haven't forgiven? Have you considered that forgiving them does not release them of their wrongdoing, but releases you from bitterness and misery? Ask God to help you forgive and to see others through His eyes.

CHAPTER 11

LAUGHTER, THE BEST MEDICINE

It's a gift to joyfully recognize and accept our own small-ness and ordinariness. Then you are free with nothing to live up to, nothing to prove, and nothing to protect. Such freedom is my best description of Christian maturity, because once you know that your 'I' is great and one with God, you can ironically be quite content with a small and ordinary 'I.' No grandstanding is necessary. Any question of your own importance or dignity has already been resolved once and for all and forever.[10]

Richard Rohr

S omething about hospital gowns and frequent exposure of all parts of your body for various tests and procedures obliterates all modesty. I've always been a very modest person, so the obvious change in my behavior (to

---

10 Richard Rohr, American author, spiritual writer, and Franciscan friar.

expose whatever needed to be exposed in the moment) was shocking and quite funny to my husband. He also noticed that I seemed oblivious to my appearance. This was the woman he had always known to be attentive to her dress, hair and makeup. Appearances were obviously not a priority in the hospital, and the results provided many moments of much needed laughter for Bob and me.

June 3, 2018

Sometimes a good laugh is what the body and soul need! Anyone who has been in a hospital building is familiar with patients walking around with their IV poles, attached by lines of various fluids. Sometimes these have to be connected 24/7. Some patients even name their poles! I am not that emotionally attached to mine! I find the pole to be quite annoying in that, every time you get up to move it has to be unplugged, with the chord looped in place so it doesn't get tangled. Then, you must maneuver the contraption into tight spaces like bathrooms and congested hallways. If you are having difficulty breathing, the added weight taxes your lungs even more. Once you get back to your bed, you must unwind the cord and plug it back into the wall outlet. Sorry, but my pole is not my friend.

Yesterday, I had gone through the process just described, many times. In the late afternoon, I was alerted that transportation was on the way to get me for a CT Scan. I commented to Bob that I needed to call the nurse to unhook my IV line so I might remove some clothing that could not be scanned. He looked at me strangely and said, "Carmen, the nurse unhooked your IV lines hours ago!"

I responded in surprise, "All this time I've lugged this thing around and you never said anything!"

He replied, "I thought you were using the pole for a walker!" We both laughed so hard! It was therapeutic for us both!

I continue to laugh about it, but it occurs to me that there is a lesson in it for me, and perhaps for you. We have such tremendous freedom in Christ. We can never earn or lose His love. When our heart is bent towards Him, we would never do anything intentionally to grieve or quench His power, or our intimacy with Him, and so He gives us more freedom to live life abundantly. But when we try to carry along the baggage from the past— our guilt, our shame, our failures—we are weighed down, needlessly! We are free! "Stand fast therefore in the liberty in which Christ has made us free, and do not be entangled again with a yoke of bondage." Galatians 5:1

My strength is increasing as the drugs win the battle over the infection. No fever today! The doctors expect another week to clear all infection, then another week to build my immune system in preparation for the CarT cells. I pray you have rested in your freedom today. Much love and thanks to you all.

CHAPTER TAKEAWAY: Laughing is therapeutic. Learning to laugh at ourselves is freeing, and gives those around you freedom to laugh with you. Life is difficult. Release your burdens and take every opportunity to lighten the load with a hearty laugh.

PERSONAL REFLECTION: Do you allow yourself to laugh? Ask God to help you see humor in your day and to share it with those around you. You may be surprised how healing a good laugh can be.

CHAPTER 12

THE VETERAN AMONG US

Flood the path with light, run our eyes to where the skies are full of promise; tune our hearts to brave music; give us the sense of community with heroes and saints of every age; and so quicken our spirits that we may be able to encourage the souls of all who journey with us on the road of life, to Your honor and glory.

St. Augustine

I was raised in the small town of Judsonia, Arkansas, population less than 2000. In 1952, a couple of years before I was born, a massive tornado ravaged the vibrant community and changed it forever. Someone driving down Main Street today would likely not be impressed. But the external doesn't describe the history, or the hearts of the men and women who raised families there, nor the wonderful people that still call Judsonia home. This is a community whose history includes being the site of one of the most destructive tornadoes in Arkansas history, but the survivors live to tell the story of rebuilding lives and overcoming brokenness.

W. E. Orr, a writer, historian, newspaper editor and columnist for the local *White County Record*, wrote a wonderful book titled, *That's Judsonia: An informal history of a small town in Arkansas.*[11] Through his writing, readers are invited to meet the people in history who passed through Judsonia, like the famous outlaw Jesse James who stayed overnight in the local hotel (which was still standing when I was a kid). Mr. Orr shares the horrifying story of the 1952 tornado including gut-wrenching first-person encounters. He introduces you to local business leaders, farmers, and average citizens. His stories spotlight the unique people who made Judsonia a community I grew to love as my hometown.

Even today, there are citizens who can tell you stories of the early days in Judsonia. Mildred Johnson Sterling, born in December of 1911, is one of those people. I spoke with her recently at the 2018, Judsonia High School "All Class Reunion." Mrs. Sterling graduated in 1928 and was honored as the oldest living alumnus at age 106! She went to college, studying music and English, and after graduating became a public school teacher and piano teacher. In fact, she was my Dad's third grade teacher!

Mrs. Sterling spent time in Washington, D.C. working as a clerk for the Department of Justice. She married and returned to Judsonia in 1946, only to lose her home and her father in the 1952 tornado. She worked in the pharmacy of a local grocery story that she and her son owned, until she

---

11 William Ewing Orr, *That's Judsonia: An informal history of a small town in Arkansas* (White Country Printing Company, 1957).

retired at age 96! Yes, If you had opportunity to turn back the pages of history to meet the citizens who were made strong by their greatest trial, you might understand why many are still proud to be "Judsonians."

I have a fascination with the stories of people—their personal history, and the events in their lives that made them who they are today. I had opportunity to hear a most fascinating story from a very unlikely source -a very frail hospital patient:

June 4, 2018

You can't judge a book by its cover. I had walked by Esther's room many times. Seeing the small, (maybe 80 lb.) lifeless form, hooked to many IV lines, including a feeding tube, I sensed she might be near her last days. I prayed silently for her as I passed her room. A couple of days ago her eyes were open when I approached her doorway, and she looked at me. I asked the nurse nearby if I might enter her room, and she said I could. I introduced myself to this frail little body, and she told me in one sentence, "I am Esther; I am 90 years old; and I have stage IV pancreatic cancer." Surprised by her alertness, I asked if I might pray for her and she said, "Please." I did, and told her I would be back to pray with her again.

When I returned the next day I asked if Esther had children. She replied that she did not, as she had never married. She had a career in the Navy! Esther pointed to a picture, she had placed in the room, of a beautiful woman in full naval uniform. So today, I spent time with Esther learning that she served from 1949–

1969 as an instructor for pilot instrument technology. All pilots went through her training during the Korean War. I immediately thought of the female character, "Charlie," in the movie Top Gun. Esther spoke of the difficulties for women in the service at that time; particularly from some commanders whom she felt did not want women serving. But Esther said she was proud to serve her country and was proud to be a woman—"Our motto was 'women first, military second.'" I asked how she coped with the difficulties and Esther replied, "Faith and prayer." What a fascinating woman inside, what appeared to be, only a frail little shell. I look forward to hearing more about the faith factor in Esther's life, as I know she will need it to carry her through this particular war. Pray for this precious veteran.

Tomorrow morning I will have a lumbar puncture to see if cancer is still evident. Efforts will continue to rid my body of infection and keep fever down. Next week, we hope for all of my blood counts to go up to non-neutropenic levels. A bone marrow aspiration will be done as an additional search for cancer cells. I still have a ways to go. Thank you for hanging with me through this journey. Your prayers are powerful!

June 6, 2018

Esther was released to a hospice facility. She told me she didn't have long. I asked about her faith and she said she is Jewish. I thanked her for allowing me to pray in Jesus' name each day. She said, "Christians have always been good to pray for my people, and my Israel." I shared how Bob and I had visited Israel twice and love the nation and its people.

I asked Esther if she was confident where she would spend eternity. She said she believed her military honors would help her get into heaven. I asked if I might share how I was confident of going to heaven. I told her that in the "New Testament" of the Bible we learn that Jesus is the Messiah, and when we look back at the "Old Testament" we can easily see the prophecies that were completely fulfilled regarding Him. I shared how Messiah Christ came, fully God and fully human, to pay a debt we couldn't pay for our sin. Only Christ could meet the criteria of a perfect sacrifice, because He alone is perfect. He is God. He chose to die on that cross, fully human, because of His amazing love for us, but He also knew the full plan. He would rise fully human, and fully God, three days later.

Hundreds witnessed Him alive, and many witnessed His ascension into Heaven where He lives today, interceding for us. Christ said that all who believe in Him have eternal life. In fact Jesus said, "Let not your hearts be troubled. Believe in God; believe also in me. In my Father's house are many rooms. If it were not so, would I have told you that I go to prepare a place for you? And if I go and prepare a place for you, I will come again and will take you to myself, that where I am you may be also." (John 14:1-3 ESV) "So my confidence, Esther, is in Christ alone, and what He did on my behalf. Our works cannot get us into Heaven, but believing in Jesus' finished work will. By believing, God declares us righteous. That frees me to serve Him out of love and thankfulness, not out of duty and fear. I can never earn His love and can never lose His love. "

I asked if she had considered Christ in that way. She said she hadn't, and that it was a fascinating story but she felt confident in her works. I pray Esther will have opportunity again to believe. The Lord reminded me "So then neither he who plants is anything, nor he who waters, but God, who gives the increase. Now he who plants and he who waters are one, and each one will receive his own reward according to his own labor, for we are God's fellow workers. . . . " 1 Corinthians 3:8–9

June 7, 2018

I must tell you of my pleasant surprise this morning! A nurse came to my room and said Esther wanted to see me! I responded, "I thought she transferred out yesterday!" The nurse said the paperwork transition took a bit longer, and she was leaving this morning. I walked into Esther's room and she had a big smile. I asked if I could hug her neck and, when she said yes, we embraced. Esther said, "I have grown to love you and I wonder if you might visit me in my new location. " Oh my goodness! Tears started rolling down my cheek. Her eyes welled with tears. I said, "If the good Lord allows, I absolutely will come see you. " I prayed for her and asked God for the opportunity to see her again. Thank you for continued prayers for Esther and for God appointments with her.

CHAPTER TAKEAWAY: If we quickly judge a person or place before we have opportunity to learn more about them, we might miss a great opportunity to hear fascinating stories that can teach us much. God orchestrates our meetings so we might learn, and so we might have opportunity to share our Jesus with others.

PERSONAL REFLECTION: Ask God to keep your eyes open for opportunities to learn from others, as well as opportunity for you to give others the hope you have in Christ!

CHAPTER 13

GOD'S GOLDEN REPAIR

Then I went down to the potter's house, and there he was, making something at the wheel. And the vessel that he made of clay was marred in the hand of the potter; so he made it again into another vessel, as it seemed good to the potter to make.

Jeremiah 18:3-4

God knows our limits and, in His grace, it seems He intersperses our difficult days with small doses of blessing, to give us hope and endurance for another day. In 2005, Bob was betrayed in a business deal and was in the process of losing his company. At the same time, he had to have neck surgery and was not able to work for nearly two years. During that time, I stepped in to run his business for 9 months, through the bankruptcy proceedings and sale of the company, while also preparing our home to sell. In all the incredible stress of our circumstances, God continued to draw us close, and to bless us regularly with small reminders of His love.

One such reminder, came through our 3- year-old grand-daughter Quinneth. On this particular day, I had literally cried all the way home from Bob's plant in Gordon, GA, to our home in Macon. It had been a difficult day dealing with angry creditors, attorneys and employees. The phone rang when I entered the house, and it was Quinneth calling who said, "I will sing to you." She began singing:

"You are my sunshine, my only sunshine.
You make me happy when skies are gray.
You'll never know dear how much I love you.
Please don't take my sunshine away."[12]

I broke down and cried as I assured Quinneth that it was the most beautiful song I had ever heard. And in that moment, it truly was. I was able to put all the cares of the day out of my mind, knowing that God loved me, was still in control, and made my phone ring that day. God's small, unexpected blessings that encourage my heart remind me that He is working to mend all that is broken -even in the midst of brokenness.

June 6, 2018

The Lord can fill a physically broken day with moments of pure joy! I had many complications yesterday, starting with efforts to draw my morning blood, and efforts to

---

12 "You are my Sunshine," 1939, written by Jimmie Davis, Charles Mitchell.

administer my needed IV antibiotics. My PICC line was taken out the day before because of complications. My veins are so very small; a team of our best nurses was in my room, with an ultrasound, to search for a usable vein. I always have Christian music playing in the morning, and as they were poking and prodding, they were singing along to their favorites. We talked about God's goodness! It was a small praise and worship service right in my room! We rejoiced with one of the nurses who shared her upcoming wedding plans and pictures of her beautiful dress! As the search for a vein continued, we laughed asking, "How many nurses does it take to change one IV line?" The search for a vein was to no avail and they wanted to stop the painful attempts, so orders were placed with the Radiology department for a new PICC line.

I was given a couple of hours to rest, and the timing was perfect. My older son's family drove in from Dallas to visit! It was such a wonderful time for this Gramma! I believe my energy soared ten levels!

My trip down to radiology for the New PICC line would also include a lumbar puncture (spinal tap) with chemo injection. The lumbar puncture was uneventful, with the most difficult part being that you must lay flat for 10 hours afterward. So while I was lying flat, efforts were made to insert the PICC line. But my left arm was infected and they found blood clots in my right arm! A temporary remedy was made while my infection heals.

And then, upon returning to my room, the Lord blessed me with a call from two precious granddaughters in Florida, a sweet surprise before bedtime. Today's physically broken moments, woven with beautiful ones, reminds me of the Japanese art of Kintsugi, whereby broken pottery is repaired with seams of gold infused lacquer, making the repaired object even more beautiful, and more valuable, than it was originally. That is what God, our Master Potter, does with our lives! He takes all of our brokenness, if we allow Him, and remakes us into another vessel, purified, and more beautiful than ever before! Thank you for your continued prayers for Bob and me as we rest in the Potter's hands!

Today was an activity-filled day! I had a head shaving (I am losing my hair a second time), a platelet transfusion, a central line placement in my chest, a nasal CT and a blood transfusion! Whew! Though each of these activities can be difficult and they were traumatic when experienced the first time, I have experienced them all before in the previous three years. Now, with each procedure there comes a sense of comfort, knowing I have an incredible medical team dedicated to making me well. I am so grateful to them and to you for praying!

CHAPTER TAKEAWAY: God sees our suffering and, in His love and grace, He steps in to provide blessing and moments of encouragement so we don't lose heart in the midst of our battle. He is continually working to repair all that is broken in our lives.

PERSONAL REFLECTION: Do you recall God's small unexpected blessings at a time when you needed encouragement? Thank God for His goodness and ask Him to keep your eyes open to His work on your behalf.

CHAPTER 14

IN MY WEAKNESS

We cannot count on God to arrange what happens in our lives in ways that will make us feel good. We can, however, count on God to patiently remove all the obstacles to our enjoyment of Him. He is committed to our joy, and we can depend on Him to give us enough of a taste of that joy and enough hope that the best is still ahead to keep us going in spite of how much pain continues to plague our hearts.[13]

Dr. Larry Crabb

It is difficult to explain the emotions experienced in the depths of suffering. Those who stand at the crossroad between death and life, who know Christ personally as Savior, understand the value of the cross that He bore on our behalf, so we might live eternally with Him. Suffering

---

13 Dr. Larry Crabb, *Shattered Dreams: God's Unexpected Path to Joy* (2001).

becomes a beautiful picture of His love for us. We begin to perceive good in all that feels so momentarily bad. This is the fellowship of His suffering.

A friend, who is mostly bedridden with Multiple Sclerosis, has taught me much about God's grace in our suffering. She shared a favorite quote of hers from a devotional book titled, *Joy and Strength*.[14] The author of the quote, dated 1842, is Henry Scott Holland:

"It is a tremendous moment when first one is called upon to join the great army of those who suffer. That vast world of love and pain opens suddenly to admit us one by one within its fortress. We are afraid to enter into the land, yet you will, I know, feel how high is the call. It is a trumpet speaking to us, that cries aloud, 'It is your turn- endure.' Play your part. As they endured before you, so now, close up the ranks—be patient and strong as they were. Since Christ, this world of pain is no accident untoward or sinister, but a lawful department of life, with experiences, interests, adventures, hopes, delights, secrets of its own. These are all thrown open to us as we pass within the gates—things we could never learn or know or see, so long as we were well. God help you to walk through this world now opened to you, as through a kingdom, royal, and wide and glorious."

My friend shared this quote in 2002, but I needed it more than ever in 2018.

---

14 Mary Wilder Tileston, *Joy & Strength*, a publication of Back to the Bible.

June 11, 2018

I was once again confined to my room today, as I don't have enough energy to walk in a stable manner, but a few feet. My fevers returned around 10:00 AM and infections have worsened. When a doctor from my oncologist team visited this morning, she said they had lined up several more tests and another platelet transfusion for me.

The oncology team's Nurse Practitioner and I have become very close. I pray for her regularly, and she sensed something different about me today. So she stayed behind, as the team went on, and asked, "What's happening?" I immediately burst into tears. She embraced me and cried with me, and said, "We are dedicated to make you well." I know they are! And I love them all dearly. I told her that the last two days had been full of bad news, and I felt so ill that I just became overwhelmed with it all. Oh I am thankful that I can cry and pray with my NP. Just releasing the tears I had held back, was therapeutic!

"SONshine," my always-bubbly PCA, came bouncing into the room later, with a big smile and a bag in her hand. Inside was a display rock that reads, "He is my Rock, my Strength, my Fortress," It was a perfect biblical phrase for me to meditate on today. Also in the bag was a beautiful necklace that says "Be Strong," and a card from the staff expressing their love for me. She said, "You minister to us every day. Now, you must let us minister to you!" Later, a nurse dropped in and said, "I know you are not Catholic, but I prayed for you at Mass, and I've brought you this Holy water." It was a beautiful vial of water, which has much meaning for my

Catholic friend and, therefore, it touched me deeply that she would bring me such a gift.

Two very special cards arrived in the mail. One was from my precious sister, Kerri. She always gives, never takes, and does not have a day without pain, due to an autoimmune disease and head and neck injuries received in previous falls. Well, she fell again and has a major concussion, yet she will be traveling from Minnesota to Arkansas this week to work on selling some items in our mother's house, to pay Mother's bills. Mother has been in a nursing home for nearly three years, and her income is taken each month for her care. I pray for Kerri's safety in the summer heat, and I pray she can accomplish what she desires, to take some of the financial burden off both our minds. And to think that she was thinking of me in sending this card!

The second card was from my dear Aunt Martha. She is in the same nursing home as my mother, but she has been there close to ten years! Paralyzed from a stroke, she cannot use her legs, or one arm, and she can't speak sentences. But she always smiles and has a phrase that she repeats over and over when you talk to her. She makes small crafts with her one good hand and gives them away to cheer up others! Oh how we all love Aunt Martha! In her beautiful card, written in childlike letters, was "I love you, Martha." Oh the Joy!

And I thought of Aunt Sue, who checks in regularly on my Mother and Aunt Martha, blessing them with meals and treats they enjoy. She just recently recovered from a third, major surgery on her jaw to correct Trigeminal

Neuralgia, which has caused non-stop pain for years. Yet she always puts others concerns before her own.

The Lord taught me today that He is always looking out for me and often blesses me through His people. And so, when I get down and have a pity party, it is ok, but don't stay there long. ! There are others with many more issues than I have. I am so blessed, and thankful for the lessons learned today! Thank you friends for your ongoing prayers and encouraging words!

CHAPTER TAKEAWAY: If we could better understand God's perspective on suffering in this world, we might fear less and trust more. If we have never experienced darkness, how can we appreciate light?

PERSONAL REFLECTION: Have you considered your trial as a "royal calling," an opportunity to learn things you could never learn when all is well? Thank God for your trial and ask Him to help you see the good and to learn all that you can in it.

CHAPTER 15

PEOPLE COME AND GO

Your response to each encounter with God determines the nature of the next encounter.[15]

Henry Blackaby

etween 1987 and 1991, Bob and I had opportunity to sit under the teaching of Dr. Forrest Lowry, our pastor at Spring Baptist Church in Spring, Texas. He took the entire congregation through foundational studies that have impacted our own lives and ministries, even to this day. We will be forever grateful. A particular favorite: *Experiencing God, Knowing and Doing the Will of God,*[16] written by Henry Blackaby. Through the seven life principles found in the study, we learned that "God is at work all

---

15 Henry Blackaby, *On Mission with God* (2002).

16 Henry Blackaby, Richard Blackaby, and Claude King, *Experiencing God* (1976).

around us" and, amazingly, "God invites us to get in on the work He is doing!" Since people and relationships are God's primary concern, we are given a tremendous opportunity to represent Him and to draw others to Christ through our love.

"But I can't reach everyone," you might say. God isn't asking us to. He gives us opportunity to influence those He places near us. Our obedience to love others, as He commands and equips us to do, allows us to experience God in a fresh way as we see lives drawn to Him. We never know the timeframe that God allows us to impact a life. People really do come and go. I knew that would be the case with the many friends I was making in the hospital. Every moment counts!

June 8, 2018

Today, Maria was released. I prayed with her this morning, and we hugged affectionately, as BFFs do. She said, "Let's do lunch on Tuesday." I will miss her, but I am told she will return in one week for her next round of Chemo. I look forward to welcoming her back! Pray for her time at home, that she will stay infection free.

My dear Muslim friend, Tina, was also released today. When she returns, it will be for a transplant. Over the past week we have had wonderful conversations about Jesus. She is a very smart young woman, and has many questions. Some questions I could answer on the spot, and others I had to research and get back to her with the answer. This morning she raised the book I had given her, Seeking Allah, Finding Jesus, and wanted me to see that she was halfway through reading it. She said if I didn't mind sharing my phone number and email, she would like to stay in touch because she knew she would have more questions. Of course I shared contact information with her!

I asked Tina if I might pray for her. After she positively responded, I asked God to protect her from infection as she awaits the transplant, and asked that He use the transplant to heal her. I prayed for her family, particularly her young daughter. I closed by asking God to open Tina's mind and heart to the truth He wants her to know about Jesus.

She asked if she could pray for me and I said, "Yes." She asked Jesus to heal me, and asked that He help her to know what is true. I have no doubt our friendship will be eternal, so I will continue to pray to that end, that she will soon grasp the reality of our Savior and the simplicity of the gospel message. Please keep praying for Tina.

Personally, I am dealing with fevers, bronchitis and continued weakness today. I had another chest X-ray and a new, powerful antibiotic was started to combat some of the concerning symptoms. They are monitoring me closely for harmful side effects. Two blood cultures were taken and breathing treatments continue. Bless you friends and family for your continued love and prayers for Bob and me.

CHAPTER TAKEAWAY: God is always at work, and what a privilege to get in on His good work. We

can be assured that His work is always about people, and the relationships we build for His purposes.

PERSONAL REFLECTION: Do you consider every encounter as an appointment from God? Have you prayed for God to show you how to invest into the lives of people you meet?

CHAPTER 16

THE NEW NORMAL

Are you prepared to let God take you into total oneness with Himself, paying no more attention to what you call the great things in life?[17]

Oswald Chambers

Coming to grips with the many changes that take place in your life and lifestyle before and after a bone marrow transplant can be emotionally overwhelming. You are forced to consider the reality of what those changes will mean to you and to your family. With Leukemia, your immune system is pretty much destroyed, and infection is the most common cause of death. Every precaution is given to avoid even a common cold or allergy issue.

---

17 Oswald Chambers, *My Utmost for His Highest* (Dodd & Mead Publishers, 1935).

Before a transplant, patients wear paper, filtered masks and, sometimes, latex gloves when outside of your hospital room.

Following the transplant, after up to 30 days in isolation, a large rubber mask with filter is required, not only in the hospital but also anywhere outside of the hospital, for up to three months. You must avoid places where people gather. So restaurants, movie theaters, malls, airports, planes, and even churches are places you must avoid. You have to steer clear of children, or the elderly in nursing homes, which for me, meant limited visits with my grandchildren and my mother.

For Bob and me, the changes included finding a place to live. We had an unresolved mold issue in our home, and I had doctors' orders not to return there, ever.

My friend Janell, whom I knew from a Bible study I taught, invited us to stay with her until we made other arrangements. We are grateful for her kindness and hospitality over a three-month period. Soon after leaving her home, we moved to an apartment in the medical center area of Houston in order to be within 15 minutes of the hospital, again, as directed by doctors.

The apartment, found after an in-depth search by my friend Beryl, and graciously made available at a discounted rate through *Kingwood Church of Christ's* apartment ministry, became our home for the following 6 months. Many of our material possessions were lost due to the mold infestation in our home, so we were most grateful that the apartment was furnished. By this point, material possessions were at the bottom of our priority list. Letting go of possessions was not difficult, but the limited interactions with those we love most, was truly the most difficult part of this journey.

I learned from a fellow patient that sometimes those loved ones with whom cancer patients are separated from include furry friends:

June 12, 2018

"But this I call to mind, and therefore I have hope: The steadfast love of the Lord never ceases; His mercies never come to an end; they are new every morning; great is Your faithfulness." Lamentations 3:21-23 (ESV)

I went to bed last night with this scripture on my mind. I so earnestly prayed that today, I would see His fresh mercies. For me that meant allowing me to get out of the room to meet a couple of new patients. I woke up with no fever! And a platelet transfusion gave me a fresh burst of energy, so I was Okayed to go!

I saw Sandy sitting in the family room weeping. I walked in and sat beside her and asked if I could help. She said that she should be happy, as she is in remission and has a donor ready for her Bone Marrow Transplant. I responded, "That is wonderful news! It sounds like God has answered prayers for you!" She agreed, but said her life would never be the same again. She is a veterinarian and, at home, she has 9 cats and 3 dogs! Her doctors told her she could not live with animals or continue her practice until she was fully released, as the animals could easily cause an infection resulting in a relapse. She loves her pets like children, and she loves her business.

I told Sandy that sometimes God allows us to lose precious things, only to replace them with something better. I said perhaps there is a wonderful new career opportunity for her. "No eye has seen, no ear has heard, and no mind has imagined what God has prepared for those who love him, " I said. I asked if she believed God's promises. She smiled and said, " Oh yes, I'm a Christian. " We talked about our faith and how God has a plan and purpose for us, much bigger than what we can see with our eyes, and by focusing on Him and submitting to His plan He brings it all to fruition, for the praise of His glory! Pray for Sandy's next great adventure, and for comfort in her losses.

I would appreciate personal prayers, specifically, for the fevers that have started again this evening, answers for the persistent cough, for blood counts to begin to rise, and for surgery scheduled at 8:00 AM tomorrow to remove a large abscess in a most difficult area! I rest in knowing I have such a supportive prayer team traveling this journey with me. You are loved! I think Lamentations 3:21–23 will be my focus again tonight!

CHAPTER TAKEAWAY: Learning to lightly hold on to all that God has given us, allows us to let go freely when it is necessary for us to do so. Recognize that this world is not our home. We are simply passing through.

PERSONAL REFLECTION: Is there anything in your life that you are not willing to let go? Ask God to decrease your affection for those things, and to increase your affection for Him and His purposes in your life.

CHAPTER 17

ONLY BY HIS GRACE

It makes no matter where He places me, or how. That is rather for Him to consider than for me; for in the easiest positions He must give me His grace, and in the most difficult, His grace is sufficient.

Hudson Taylor

God often teaches us life lessons that He desires for us to remember for our lifetime. Sometimes those lessons are learned from friends who experienced a similar trial and were faithful to bring honor and glory to the Lord during their difficult days. Such was the case of two very dear friends I lost to cancer in 2000 and 2002, both in their early 30's.

I learned much from Andrea and Kate. Andrea worked for me in Washington, D.C., and Kate was her roommate. Andrea was also in my home Bible study. A couple of years before joining the study she was diagnosed with lung cancer and had a lung transplant, but had relapsed. The other young women in the study and I ministered to Andrea, offering practical helps like doing her laundry and taking her to Chemo treatments to hold her hand. We all prayed regularly for her. We were heartbroken to lose her. We were also grateful that her suffering had ended, knowing she was healed completely in the presence of her Savior.

We were excited to have Kate join us in our Bible study soon after. She had many questions about her grief and anger toward God for taking her friend so young. And then, we were all shocked and heartsick to learn that Kate was diagnosed with colon cancer. Our practices of loving on Andrea now transferred to Kate, and we grieved losing this beautiful young friend, as well. She was a newlywed and longed to be a mom. It was difficult to grasp God's purposes in taking both of these women so soon. I grieved for both, long after their passing. But we could all say that these brilliant, young attorneys taught us all life lessons as they fought their toughest battles with pure grace.

In my Bible, I have noted, "Lessons learned from Kate: Focus on others, not self; be a better listener; give life to life, not death; be bold for Christ with love and grace."

And, elsewhere in my Bible, "Lessons learned from Andrea: Don't let aches and pains keep you from living life to its fullest; have an eternal perspective to determine what is really important in this life; don't ever waste God's mercy."

Yes, these two women taught me much about suffering and dying, but more importantly, about living. Thinking of them helps me to stay focused and to not let bumps in the road steal my joy for life. I realize that God is still touching my life through the memories of these precious young ladies, and in their honor, I can practice the lessons they taught me, so others may receive God's touch through me.

June 13, 2018

Some days are "hurry up and wait" kind of days. I was prepared at 6:00 AM for 8:00 AM surgery. Perhaps you have had the NPO orders before surgery, which means no food or drink after midnight. But after checking my blood, I had to have both a blood and platelet transfusion, so my surgery was delayed to 10:30 AM.

I contacted sweet friends who had planned to drive quite a distance to visit, to let them know of the delay and that the scheduled 12:30 PM visit would probably not work. At 10:30 AM my temperature was over 100 and needed to be below 100 for the surgery. So, I was given a Tylenol, and a much-needed sip of water for the fever, and told we would reschedule for 12:30 PM surgery. Blood was taken again to see how my counts were doing. My platelets were low, so at 1:30 PM I had another platelet transfusion. They tell me 4:00 PM is my new surgery time!

I realize now, in frustration, that my friends could have visited after all. But once again, God is speaking to my heart. I so often want to control how my day goes. I have my routines and like to see things happen as planned, in order. But insisting that God, or others, follow my plan instead of a better plan, limits what God intends to do in those situations. My anxiety when my plan is not "falling into place" brings no honor to Him. Forgive me Lord! "But those who wait on the Lord shall renew their strength; They shall mount up with wings like eagles, they shall run and not be weary, they shall walk and not faint." (Isaiah 40:31) Bless you for your Prayers! My transport to surgery has arrived!

CHAPTER TAKEAWAY: It is easy to get caught up in the culture's demand for immediate satisfaction and self-focus, but God desires we stay focused on Him, learn at His feet, and live with His purposes and eternity always in sight.

PERSONAL REFLECTION: Are circumstances and the demands of each day causing restlessness and anxiety in your life? Ask God to help you refocus on what is important to Him, and to be content to have it so.

CHAPTER 18

IT'S A SMALL WORLD

You have enclosed me behind and before, and laid Your hand upon me. Such knowledge is too wonderful for me; It is too high, I cannot attain it.

Psalm 139:5-6 (NASB)

I am often pleasantly surprised when I cross paths with people I knew from years past, who suddenly appear in my life again. I am beginning to see that all of our encounters are orchestrated by God. When someone comes back into our life, there are perhaps purposes yet unfulfilled in our friendship, or in the plans God has for our combined gifts and talents. Sometimes, God has an opportunity for us, and reconnecting with people in our past is the open door.

When I worked in Washington D.C., I was a guest on many radio programs that aired across the nation. One of those programs, on which I was a frequent guest, was *Point of View*, at the time hosted by the founder of the program,

Marlin Maddoux. After leaving the nation's Capitol in 2002, those guest appearances eventually ended.

In 2005, when I was running my husband's plant in Gordon, GA through the bankruptcy, and sale of the plant and our home, we did not know what we would do for an income following that particular trial. It would be another year before Bob could work again, and I wasn't sure where to start a job search. But as God would have it, I received a call at the plant from a familiar voice. It was Marlin's wife, Mary.

Mary had always produced *Point of View* and, in that role, she was the person who would contact me to be a guest on the show. I was so surprised to hear from her and asked, "Mary, how in the world did you find me?"

She replied, "Oh, God knew where to find you."

Sadly, she had called, first of all, to let me know that Marlin had passed away the previous year. She was now looking for someone to co-host the program with Kerby Anderson, and wondered if I might consider a move to Dallas, to take that position. I knew God had answered our prayers! I was beyond thrilled and agreed to the offer. God is so faithful. God quickly found a buyer for our home and we moved to Dallas, where I enjoyed working with *Point of View* for the next 5 years.

Fast forward to 2013. Bob and I were living in San Antonio, TX at the time. One Sunday morning in church, as we were standing to greet the folks around us, the person behind us was a very familiar face. In fact, we both shouted as we embraced. Christy had worked with me at *Point of View*, as an assistant in production. I loved this sweet girl, but had lost track of her. On this particular Sunday, Christy and her husband Dave were visiting the church, as they had just recently moved to the area. Dave was newly in remission from Non-Hodgkin Lymphoma, and Christy had taken a job nearby. Our friendship was rekindled and, to this day, we remain dear friends. God has allowed us to work on projects together, and she and Dave offered incredible support during my cancer battle. God never ceases to amaze.

Sometimes, those *small world* encounters come about as direct answers to our prayers. As we desire that God touch others through us, He provides opportunities that will make that happen. But, I never anticipated another *small world* encounter in the Radiology department:

June 16, 2018

It's a small world, and God is all over it! I have been praying about how to get to know Donna, as she is very guarded in her conversation. Yesterday morning, after my blood work was complete, my new PICC line quit working— both lines! Because all of my antibiotics are given through the line, I was immediately scheduled to have the line replaced in Radiology.

Arriving in Radiology, there is much preparation for surgery procedures, as many of you well know! In my case, I had at least 30 minutes before the Fentanyl kicked in. Though a pain med, it makes me very drowsy. But, the two nurses attending me both had bubbly personalities and conversation flowed! I learned they were both from Louisiana, originally, and one had lived in Baton Rouge, where my husband and I had lived for 3 years. So there was much conversation about the "best shrimp Po-boys," the "best beignets," LSU loyalty and the churches where we worshipped.

One of the nurses asked about my cancer, and what the medical plan was for me. I shared and she said, "My aunt has ALL (Acute Lymphoblastic Leukemia) and is on your floor. I asked, "What is her name? I probably know her."

When she replied, "Donna," I almost fell off the table! She spent our remaining time telling me about Donna.

As she spoke I was listening, but at the same time, I was thinking, "Wow God, You are indeed all knowing, all powerful, and everywhere present!" Don't underestimate how God is able to coordinate circumstances, people, and time to answer our prayers for His good purposes! I am now better prepared to have meaningful conversations with Donna.

I am anticipating a great Saturday with Bob. I am free of fever, and progress is being made in other areas of concern! God is hearing your prayers and Bob and I remain humbled and grateful!

CHAPTER TAKEAWAY: God orchestrates every encounter. He is always working on behalf of His children and allows us to come together in love and unity to accomplish His purposes.

PERSONAL REFLECTION: Are there people whose path you have crossed more than once, and at unexpected times and places? Ask God to show you His purposes in those encounters, and how you might be of service to those you meet, or how you might serve together.

CHAPTER 19

LAY YOUR BURDENS DOWN

Oh mystery of grace, that chose me to stand before Your face, to be Your special measure, Your portion, Your delight, Your own; that takes pleasure in me who fears Your name, who hopes alone in Your sweet mercy's boundless store.

Frances Ridley Havergal[18]

Among the many burdens that come with a disease, like cancer, are the extremely large medical bills. Additional costs incurred with your treatment include transportation and parking for outpatient visits, or for a visiting spouse; and additional housing costs when you must live near the medical center. According to the National Cancer Institute, between 33% and 80% of cancer

---

18 Frances Ridley Havergal, (1836-1879) English poet and hymn writer, best known for the hymn, "Take My Life and Let it Be."

survivors exhaust their savings to finance medical expenses. For those who fall into debt, the level of debt is substantial. "The problem of paying for cancer care is so vast that it has a name, financial toxicity, representing the *other* toxic side effect of cancer treatment. Patients who get into financial difficulty suffer high rates of emotional distress and lower quality of life."[19]

The burden is very real, but God desires that we lay this burden at His feet. As He allows us to experience trials, even the magnitude of cancer, we can count on Him to provide for our financial needs. I am so very grateful that much of our provision has come through Bob's employment and his company's excellent healthcare benefits. We don't take that blessing lightly, and grieve for those who have no healthcare coverage.

Our additional costs have been covered, in part, through medical discounts and through organizations like the *American Cancer Society,* and *The Leukemia Society of Texas.* Parking discounts are made available through the Methodist Hospital patient services. God gives us wisdom and motivation to seek out the resources available to assist us. No doubt there are some we missed. For the substantial balances still owed, we have found favor when we contact the billing offices. Either they can discount the balance further, or help in setting up a payment plan.

But always, we give thanks ahead of time for the provision we know God will make in His way and in His time. There is no need for us to worry. "*Can any one of you by worrying*

---

19 STAT News, November 2, 2016, "Financial Toxicity: 1 in 3 Cancer patients have to turn to friends or family to pay for care," by Scott D. Ramsey and Veena Shankaran.

add a single hour to your life?" (Matthew 6:27) God has shown Himself faithful again and again.

One such provision came in February of 2018. We anticipated getting money back from the IRS, and so we filed early in hopes of receiving money to pay toward some of the medical bills. But to our surprise, we owed money instead—just over $2000! As we were driving home disheartened, we began discussing God's faithfulness, and thanked Him for how He might provide money to pay our taxes.

The phone rang, even as we talked. The caller was a representative from our previous mortgage company. He asked to confirm our new address as he had an escrow refund for us. In high hopes, I asked how much it would be. He replied, "$2000." Yes, we can give God our financial burdens. He is always working on our behalf, and He wants us to tell others of His goodness.

June 17, 2018

I am so thankful for a blessed day, in so many ways! This morning a nurse came by and told me that Donna was really nervous, and they weren't sure why. She asked if I might drop by her room. I asked the Lord to give me ears to hear and words to speak, if necessary.

I went into her room and her husband Doug was there. Strangely, I had met him at the coffee counter, and had discussed his loved one who was ill. I had prayed for her, but had not been able to make the connection with Donna. Donna thanked me for coming, and I asked why she was particularly troubled today. She said she was very nervous about a round of Chemo she was about to get, as the last time she had this particular Chemo, she became very ill. She also said that she had not slept in days, worried about hospital bills. So we talked about both concerns.

I first addressed some practical helps for the financial issues, having dealt with most of the billing problems that arise when you have been ill for almost 3 years! She and Doug were thankful to know the steps to take to follow up with insurance coverage; how to get the billing department's patient advocates involved; and how to set up payment plans with each billing entity.

But then, we talked about the root issue of both concerns: worry. I shared how I try to give all of my worries to the Lord. The last thing we need when trying to heal, is stress, caused by needless worry. I talked about how God made her, loves her, and knows her every need. The whole time I am talking, Doug is nodding his head in agreement.

I asked if I could pray and they both said, "Please do." As I prayed, I reinforced the gospel message, and asked God to hear our prayers for Donna's concerns. I also asked God to bless the wonderful nurses and PCA's who care for us every day, who love us so much, and asked that He help us to be extra kind to them and to take an interest in their lives, to be a blessing, not a burden.

Later, two nurses came to my room smiling. One said, "Miss Pate, have you been talking to Miss Donna?" I told them I had and asked why. One replied, "Because today is the first time she smiled, asked how our day was going, and wanted to know about our families!" They decided I must have been talking to her. God is so good. That visit with Donna was totally of Him.

I am feeling so well today and look forward to a great night's sleep! Thank you all for praying for my friends, and for Bob and me.

CHAPTER TAKEAWAY: God sees and knows your every need, even before you ask for His help. He desires we recognize Him as our faithful provider, and trust Him to meet our financial needs in His way and in His timing.

PERSONAL REFLECTION: Have you thanked God for His faithful provision in your life? Do you ask in faith, for God to meet your immediate needs? Ask Him now to give you His peace in the waiting.

CHAPTER 20

DON'T LOSE HEART

Therefore, whether you eat or drink, or whatever you do, do all to the glory of God.

1 Corinthians 10:31

It seems one can muster enough strength, faith and spiritual joy for a battle. But it is more difficult to maintain the same level of strength, faith, and joy in the daily grind of life, particularly when you are a patient, and your "daily grind" is in a hospital for an extended period of time. Your daily routine is pretty much confined to the floor of your hospital wing, and most often to your room. In most cases, your window view is of the building across the street, and you can't see the sky unless you go to the window and look straight up. The meals become monotonous after a couple of weeks, when every item on the menu has been tried, at least twice. Without the proper perspective, routine vital checks, medicine delivery, and myriad of tests and treatments become a source of dread.

A favorite book of mine in helping to gain proper perspective on circumstances is *Balancing the Christian Life*[20] by Dr. Charles C. Ryrie. In a chapter he titles, "Routine Faithfulness," he reminds readers that the basis for a Christian's judgment before Christ is faithfulness, and that is why it is required of stewards that a man be found faithful. And, if we consider our lives, we will quickly realize that most of our activity is in the daily routine of life, not in the grandiose affairs.

Dr. Ryrie wrote, "We all tend to let our guard down in the routine. And if the same routine is our lot for very long we inevitably grow weary and often disheartened simply because the routine gets us down." But, he reminds us, if biblical principles of spiritual living work at all, they certainly should work in the routine of life. According to Dr. Ryrie, there are four areas that need our focus or we will lose heart:

1. Faithfulness in problems—we must commit our problems to God and patiently wait for His solutions. The apostle Paul found himself in prison more often than not, but he assured himself with the promise that God renews the inward man daily, even though the outward man is subject to all kinds of pressures and problems.

2. Faithfulness in prayer—In the parable found in Luke 18 of the persistent widow and the unjust judge, we can find three promises concerning prayer. First, we have a heavenly Father who cares intimately for those who come to Him. Second,

---

20 Charles C. Ryrie, *Balancing the Christian Life* (1969), 107.

we are God's elect with all of the privileges that such a relationship brings, including being an heir of all things. And third, He will see that the answer comes and justice will be done, suddenly, in His timing. So don't lose heart in prayer!

3. Faithfulness in good works—It is about imitating Christ who "went about doing good." (Acts 10:38) Loving others with an encouraging word is a good work and that can be done- even from a hospital bed.

4. Faithfulness in witness—Two reasons to be intentional about sharing the gospel message: It is a message of life, liberty, and transforming power. Secondly, we ourselves have experienced this transforming power, and since we know personally what the gospel can do, we are impelled to tell others.

If we practice these areas consistently, we won't lose heart in the daily grind of life. In fact, we will find joy along the way.

June 18, 2018

A PCA came by and asked, "Did you know Miss Maria is back?" I told her I didn't.

She laughed and said Miss Maria wondered why her best friend hadn't been by, but immediately asked, "What's her name?"

So I went down and asked, "Maria, do you remember me?"

She said, "Of course I do, I've known you for 40 years. But why did you cut off your hair?"

I told her it began to fall out while she was gone and I had my head shaved. "So now we look alike," I said smiling.

She smiled, but quickly said, "Well, just take a friend's advice, you look better with hair. I think you should grow it back!"

I said, "I will Maria, just for you, but it will take a long time."

She said, "Well, you shouldn't have cut it all off."

I prayed for her next round of Chemo, and told her that God and I love her! And we do!

I had opportunity to meet Sandy's parents. (Sandy is the veterinarian who had to give up her pets.) They will help her get an apartment close to her home, so that she will have opportunity to make short visits to see her beloved pets. They will actually care for the animals so she is not exposed more than she should be. Sandy seemed so relieved and excited about that arrangement. I said, "Well, let's just thank God for that plan!" And we did.

Donna and I walked together a couple of times today. I wish I could explain the beautiful difference in her countenance. In fact, when we connected for our first walk, she was picking up a stack of "I Noticed You" cards from the nurses station. The cards are meant for patients use, to acknowledge the good deeds we might observe from hospital staff.

Donna asked, "Have you seen these?" I told her I had, and use them frequently. She said, "I've never noticed these before. I have a lot of catching up to do."

> My time with Bob was special, as always. Some may wonder why we sit here with quiet music playing, and sometimes don't say a word. After 32 years of marriage, just being together brings joy to us both. But tomorrow I will beat him in a game of Cribbage!

CHAPTER TAKEAWAY: Since most of our life is spent in daily routine, looking for the good in our day, and enjoying the blessings we are given, help us to stay faithful in prayer, in our problems, in good works, and in our witness.

PERSONAL REFLECTION: How do you view your daily routine—as dull and with dread? Ask God to help you see the blessing in every day. Look for good works you might do for others and for opportunities to reflect Christ.

CHAPTER 21

JUST FOR A SEASON

The greatest danger facing all of us is that we may fail to perceive life's greatest meaning, fall short of its highest good, miss its deepest and most abiding happiness, be unable to render the most needed service, be unconscious of life ablaze with the light of the Presence of God—and be content to have it so.[21]

Phillips Brooks

It is true that seasons come and go in a lifetime. We have all experienced a season of childhood and carefree days, and a season of young adulthood where we focused on our education or careers. Many experience the joy of marriage and a season of childbearing. But then the children grow up and leave home, and we realize how short was the

---

21 *Sermons by Phillips Brooks* (New York: E.P. Dutton and Company,1893).

parenting season. A spouse dies and we experience the grief of a marriage that ended too soon, and enter a new season of widowhood.

The Psalmist David rightly said, *Weeping may endure for a night, but joy comes in the morning.* (Psalm 30:5b) David understood that our difficult circumstances don't last and, therefore, we can always be hopeful for good days ahead. As I consider the many trials God has brought Bob and me through, none of them lasted a lifetime, though in the moment of those trials we may have felt they surely would. Only when we understand that there is joy to be found in the difficult seasons, and there are lessons for us to learn there, do we seize the opportunity to grow and to serve where God has placed us.

Sometimes we have to step back and prayerfully evaluate our situation. How might I honor God as I walk through this trial? Is God trying to touch someone's life through me? What are the lessons He is trying to teach me? Am I obedient to the Holy Spirit's nudging to love and serve others? Am I faithful to seek God for wisdom and discernment? Only God can help us with the answers to these questions. But when we trust His leading, our troubles will soon be replaced with the joy we were seeking all along. We will have His strength to carry us through till the morning comes.

June 18, 2018

Unexpected twists and turns are often opportunities to get in on God's work! I felt well this morning and looked forward to my early walk, followed by my coffee reward (1500 steps =1 large coffee). When I arrived at the coffee station, I recognized a young woman there as the caretaker of the sweet elderly woman who is a patient on my hallway.

The patient arrived a few days ago, and I had not yet stopped by Miss Bonnie's room to introduce myself. So, at the coffee station I met Miss Bonnie's daughter, Stacia. I asked about her mom and how I might pray for her. She asked that I please pray that her mom's faith does not give out. "Her faith is strong, but she is so tired and weak."

I told her I would pray as she asked and that I would visit her mom later. I then asked how I might pray for Stacia, and her eyes filled with tears. She said she was tired also, and that she needs direction regarding her mom's needs, and the competing needs of her own family. In addition to caring for all of her family, Stacia has a job and also goes to school! She said, "I want to honor God, but I honestly don't know what He wants me to do right now!"

I prayed with Stacia and asked God to show her what she might let go of in this particular season. I asked Him to help her find much needed rest. After praying, I asked if it had occurred to her that her mom is receiving excellent care, 24/7, from God and the medical team here. Perhaps she does not also need to be here as much as she thinks. I also suggested she might consider putting her classes on hold for now, as she probably finds focusing on her classes very difficult in her current situation. She agreed, and I told her I would continue to pray for both her and her mom. ". . . For your Father knows exactly what you need even before you ask him!" Matthew 6:8(NLT)

I was whisked away, right after my morning doctor visit, for another CT Scan and a Lumbar Puncture with Chemo, requiring me to lie flat for 10 hours afterward, so I did not get over to Miss Bonnie's room today. I appreciate prayers for resolution to my cough and breathing issues. The CT revealed a lung infection. Please pray also for good results from the Lumbar Puncture. Thank you for your continued support in this journey.

CHAPTER TAKEAWAY: Different seasons of our lives bring various opportunities to learn, grow and mature. Often times we take on commitments and activities that God intended we hold off for another season. Discerning priorities for the season we are in can help reduce the burden and stress in our lives.

PERSONAL REFLECTION: Ask God to clarify the season you are in, and to help you in setting aside activities and commitments that can wait for another time. Be content with your season and learn everything God has planned for you in it.

CHAPTER 22

THE JOY OF THE LORD

Our spiritual life cannot be measured by success as the world measures it, but only by what God pours through us—and we cannot measure that at all.

Oswald Chambers

How am I to maintain a countenance of joy in the midst of doubt, uncertainty, and stress of the day—even in the all-consuming battle with illness? I am learning to do so by focusing on all that I know is true, and certain. The apostle Paul, writing from prison, charged, *Finally, brethren, whatever things are true, whatever things are noble, whatever things are just, whatever things are pure, whatever things are lovely, whatever things are of good report, if there is any virtue and if there is anything praiseworthy— meditate on these things.* (Philippians 4:8)

I find it helpful to also focus on our many blessings: the prayers that have been answered; the many who pray for us, literally around the world; our children, Jason and his wife Jessica, Josh and his wife Michelle, Holly, and grandchildren—Sydney, Sarah, Emily, Quinneth, Lyndon, Anson, Molly and Makayla—who all give us tremendous joy; opportunities to serve no matter where God places us; and the daily joy of being alive, knowing God isn't finished with me yet.

Nearly 30 years ago, I wrote a life mission statement: "To help others be all that God designed them to be, regardless of their past or present circumstances." To that end, I have tried to be intentional over the years, to offer the gifts and talents God has given me to encourage others where God has placed them, and to help them to see their God-given potentials. I make their expressed dreams and passions a matter of prayer, asking God to make His calling on their lives clear to them. I was particularly grateful to hear of an answered prayer during this hospital stay.

June 19, 2018

Deciding on a career choice? Nurses and PCAs are needed! I have been praying heavily today for God to send help to the hospitals! One reason the staff works such long hours is there is a shortage of nurses and PCAs. Last night there was only one PCA on our floor, for about 20 patients. Today, with bands of tropical storm rains coming into Houston, three nurses could not get to work. I could see the stress on the faces of the nurses here, and one explained the situation. As I have walked around today, I have silently prayed for each one. I never heard one complain, and they all smiled and did their jobs with excellence! Please join me in praying that more young people will consider if they are called and gifted to enter this vital field of care!

I was lying in my room this afternoon, with my door open. Transportation was picking up a patient across the hall. The transporter caught my eye, and said, "Hi Miss Pate! Do you remember me?" I did remember Derrick! He had transported me numerous times when I was here last year, but not this time around.

He had shared with me, back then, how he would be the first in his family to graduate college, but he didn't know what he wanted to do afterward. He was working on a science degree.

I told Derrick today that I did remember him well, because we had talked about his gifts and passion. I asked how school was going, and he said he had earned a BA, and was now continuing his education. I asked if God had given him any direction, career wise.

Derrick smiled and said, "Yes Mam, I'm going to be a nurse!" God is already answering my prayers!

Today I struggled with breathing and coughing, but some changes were made to medications, and hopefully the issue will be resolved soon! Thank you for ongoing prayers and love! Bob and I so appreciate each of you.

CHAPTER TAKEAWAY: Keeping our focus on what is true; counting our blessings daily; and living out our purpose and calling bring great joy that can carry us through difficult days.

PERSONAL REFLECTION: Have you stopped to count your many blessings today? Use your gifts and talents to fulfill your passion and focus on all that you know to be true. Watch to see how quickly joy replaces fear, doubt and uncertainty.

CHAPTER 23

IT'S A GOD THING

Your unfailing love is better than life itself; how I praise You! I will praise You as long as I live, lifting up my hands to You in prayer. You satisfy me more than the richest feast. I will praise You with songs of joy. I lie awake thinking of You, meditating on You through the night. Because You are my helper, I sing for joy in the shadow of Your wings. I cling to You; Your strong right hand holds me securely.

Psalm 63:3-8 (NLT)

Bob and I remain in awe of God's goodness. He truly does provide for His kids, and we have been the beneficiaries of His faithful and abundant provision. In an earlier chapter, I mentioned our friend Dr. Sumner Wemp, the retired professor from Liberty University. Bob was a student of Dr. Wemp, and I also had opportunity to take one of his courses.

Years later, while working and living in the Dallas area, we made a point to reach out to Dr. Wemp and his beautiful wife, Celeste, as they had retired there. We enjoyed their company and had opportunity to pray for them, and they for us. Our friendship grew over time but, sadly for us, Celeste passed on to glory.

Not long after, I was laid off from my job with *Point of View Radio Talk Show*. One day at lunch with Dr. Wemp, he expressed to Bob and me that he was struggling living alone, and though he would go live near his children in Arizona at some point, he was not ready to make the transition. His kids had provided home health care and housekeeping services, but he felt he needed live-in help.

After leaving Dr. Wemp that day, I told Bob I felt we were to offer to move in with him and take care of him until he was ready to go to Arizona. Our lease was ending on our apartment and since I was unemployed, I could focus on caring for Dr. Wemp. Bob agreed. We discussed the arrangement with Dr. Wemp, and he loved the idea. After getting the blessing of his children, we moved in.

We covered all of the expenses for food and any increases in utilities. I cleaned, did grocery shopping, cooked, took Dr. Wemp to doctor appointments, and made sure he took all of his medications, as prescribed. He, in turn, allowed us to live with him rent-free.

Only a week after moving in, the company where Bob worked burned to the ground, so Bob and other employees were let go. We are still in awe of the fact that God knew beforehand that we would both be without jobs, and would need a place to live that was affordable for us, until we found employment. We knew that God had made these living arrangements for us. His provision was perfect during the months that we lived with Dr. Wemp.

In addition, we had opportunity to learn much from this man of God. Never underestimate how God works behind the scenes to meet your every need, and His purposes in your life, when your heart's desire is for Him and His glory.

June 20, 2018

God gave me such favor today, and I want you to know what an awesome God we serve! Our insurance company covers 30 consecutive days in a hospital facility and then, you must be sent home for a week, or longer, before returning for another 30 day covered stay. Today was Day 30, and yet the doctors did not feel I was ready to go home because of breathing issues and surgical wound care needs. My wonderful doctors and social workers began working diligently this morning to come up with a solution.

Well, as God would have it, there is a brand new transitional facility a few miles from the hospital. It is a state of the art, luxurious facility with all the bells and whistles. The facility holds 70 patients and currently they have only 15. The facility has desired a partnership with Houston Methodist, to receive patients in transition. So, the hospital has asked me to go there for 10 days, while I heal, and to evaluate the care and services of the facility, for the hospital! Is that incredible, or what? I have been praising the Lord all afternoon for His faithfulness and goodness. An ambulance will transport me there in a couple of hours. And to top off that huge blessing, the staff presented me with a Certificate of Appreciation. All on duty signed the back with words of encouragement and love. I have been hugging necks and shedding tears of gratefulness for each one!

I had a bone marrow biopsy today and results should be in early next week. From there, we will determine if I return here for more chemo, or to the transplant center for CarT cells. How could I not trust God with His plan after today's blessings? Deuteronomy 7:9 says, "Know therefore that the LORD your God is God, the faithful God who keeps covenant and steadfast love with those who love him and keep his commandments, to a thousand generations." What a great promise for all of us to cling to! Much love and thankfulness for joining me on this journey!

CHAPTER TAKEAWAY: God knows your every need and is always working behind the scenes to look out for you. He sees the big picture while we only see present circumstances. He moves people and resources to work together for your good.

PERSONAL REFLECTION: Are your circumstances causing you anxiety because you don't have solutions? Have you asked God to direct your steps and to help you along the way? Rest in His care and watch for God to work on your behalf.

CHAPTER 24

HEART IMPRINTS

So, affectionately longing for you, we were well pleased to impart to you not only the gospel of God, but also our own lives, because you had become dear to us.

1 Thessalonians 2:8

There is a quote, by an author unknown to me, which says, "Some people come quickly into our lives and leave, while some stay awhile leaving footprints on our hearts and we are never the same." I think of so many wonderful people who have left footprints on my heart. But a group of people, who cared for me and looked out for me during many transitions in my personal life, was my Kroger family. I worked for the Kroger Company for seventeen years, starting as a checker in a store in Searcy, Arkansas. I transferred to Houston as a single mom of two boys, and after a second failed marriage, my Kroger co-workers became my family.

Soon after moving to Houston, I was promoted to Kroger's division office where I worked in operations and, then, became the Consumer Affairs Manager for the Texas/Louisiana Division. It was a wonderful company to work for as they invested heavily in the training and development of their employees. In fact, during those years, Kroger had an education center where I had the opportunity to take management courses including, but not limited to, model management, crisis management and customer relations. It was through Kroger that I gained extensive media training and had opportunity to put my new skills to work with local media.

By far my greatest memories, however, are of the people- from the store employees to the division office staff and management. Such great friendships were built. Together, we *gave back* to the communities we served through assistance to local food banks and pantries; fundraisers and fun runs for various charities, and even planting trees to beautify the communities. I grew to love my Kroger co-workers.

Although I left the company in 1991, I still think of the many I knew during those days as part of my extended family. They have been among my most faithful prayer warriors during my cancer journey. Quarterly, there is a get-together for those who have retired from Kroger, and they have been kind to include me. What a blessing to see familiar faces, to hug necks, and to reminisce the "good old days" of our Kroger years.

Every encounter has the potential of becoming a heart imprint for you and for the person you meet. When we are open to loving others and entering their world, the impact can be for a lifetime. I know that will be the case with the many I encountered at Methodist Hospital. Now

God was giving me additional opportunities at the Houston Transitional Center.

June 21, 2018

New faces bring new opportunities! It was bittersweet leaving my hospital "family," but I know I will be back there soon! The ambulance team that transported me to the Transitional Center was very personable. One of the nurses commented, as they were wheeling me away, "You are taking our prayer warrior."

Andrew, the driver, picked up on that immediately and said, "Well I could use prayer!" So I asked him what was going on. He said he has just gone through a very bad break-up with a girlfriend, and he realizes now that she was not good for him. I asked him how so, and he said, "She doesn't share my faith. She doesn't have a biblical worldview, and it made our time together rough." He prays to find a woman who shares his Christian faith, so they can worship and serve God together."

I applauded him for that desire, which is certainly in line with God's will. I told him I would pray with him, that God would hear his prayers.

His coworker, Jacob, listened quietly. I asked how I could pray for him. He said, "I am a Jew. My extended family has returned to Israel, our homeland, and I would like to take my family there as well." I always get chills when a Jewish friend mentions returning to Israel. Often they will say there is a desire they can't quench. I know that God has given them that desire. There are so many biblical prophecies which speak of this, including this one:

Isaiah 43:5–7b–"Do not be afraid, for I am with you; I will bring your descendants from the east and gather you from the west. I will say to the north, `Give them up!' and to the south, `Do not hold them back.' Bring my sons from afar and my daughters from the ends of the earth—Everyone who is called by My name, whom I have created for My glory . . . ." I told Jacob I would gladly pray that God would make a way for his family to go home to Israel.

The Transitional Center is fabulous. And though there are only 15 patients in this 70-room facility, it is well staffed. I am meeting them all, patients and staff, and trying to remember names!

One patient I met is a sweetheart! Darius is 30 years old and has colon cancer. Though in a wheelchair, I could tell he was quite tall, but probably weighs less than 100 lbs. He told me he attended the University of Illinois on a basketball scholarship, but hurt his knee his 3rd year and was finished. He graduated college, however, with an MBA in business. He said his daddy worked on custom cars when he was alive, and he so desired to continue his daddy's legacy. So, he bought a custom detail shop for classic cars, and loved his work, but he had to sell his business due to his cancer.

He feels he has been dealt a bad hand, but is learning to trust God for what happens next. He said he focuses on the blessings and holds on to the promise that God "will restore what the locusts have eaten." We had a wonderful conversation about God's goodness and faithfulness and never ending love. I prayed with him and he asked if we could talk again.

I am getting the help I need for breathing and wound care, and just praise the Lord for giving me a new place to serve Him over the next 10 days! Thank you for your ongoing prayers! God is listening and answering!

CHAPTER TAKEAWAY: Every friendship has the potential of influencing one another for a lifetime. God places value on friendship and desires we reflect Him and His character to our friends. His ultimate desire is that we all would be part of His eternal family.

PERSONAL REFLECTION: How are you influencing others? Do they see Christ in you? Have you considered that your friendship with others could draw them to Jesus, or perhaps God desires you both draw closer to Him through your friendship?

CHAPTER 25

THE LOST SHEEP

Jesus leaving the ninety-nine to find one seems illogical, irrational, and senseless . . . until that one is you.

Walk FM.com

I love the parables of the lost coin, the lost sheep, and the prodigal son, as told by Christ in Luke 15. In each story, the person's loved possession was missing, or gone astray, and it was paramount for the lost to be found. There was great rejoicing when the coin was found, the sheep was recovered, and the son came home.

Through the parables, Christ illustrates God's love for the lost and His joy over the found. When the prodigal son wandered away, to live life apart from his father, his status as a son did not change. He was still a son, still part of the family, but the fellowship was broken. The father was waiting with arms open wide for his son to come back home, back to restored fellowship. What a beautiful picture of God's love for His children who go astray.

For many years, I was that prodigal. God did not give up on me through my years of wandering, though my sins were many. When I hit rock bottom, He welcomed me back with my repentant and broken heart. I cannot imagine straying again from a Father who loves me so; who demonstrated His mercy and grace again. Though I was unworthy, He restored our fellowship as His much-loved daughter. Amazing grace!

This excerpt from Dr. Dave Anderson's book, *Maximum Joy,* is a good reminder for us all to stay close to the Shepherd:

"One of my favorite paintings of Jesus is called, 'The Good Shepherd.' It pictures Christ as a shepherd out in a pastoral setting, surrounded by sheep. But what interests me most about the painting is not the Shepherd as much as the sheep. The Shepherd is holding one little lamb in His arms; a couple more are nudging up against His robe. Others are lying in a cluster not far away. Further back in the scene we see some sheep grazing. But it's the sheep far from the Shepherd who concern me. Some are looking this way and others that way. They are not at all close to the Shepherd. These are the sheep, which are in danger of the wolf. These are the sheep, which are in danger of falling off a cliff and breaking their bones. If you were doing a self-portrait to touch up this painting, where would you place yourself in the picture?"[22]

We are in daily spiritual battle friends. Stay close to the Shepherd!

Christ also speaks of those who are not yet His; they have not yet believed. He says, *I have other sheep, too, that are*

---

22 Dave Anderson, *Maximum Joy: First John—Relationship or Fellowship?* (Grace Theology Press, 2016), 107.

not in this sheepfold. I must bring them also. They will listen to my voice, and there will be one flock with one shepherd. John 10:16 (NLT) I met a man at the Transitional Center who heard the voice of the Shepherd, and what a story he had to tell:

June 22, 2018

I met Hyman in the dining room. He and I were the only two patients there, and he asked me to join him. I asked him to tell me about himself, and for 30 minutes he shared his story. A very successful, Hispanic rancher and businessman, Hyman said he had it all. And having it all led to alcohol, drug addiction and womanizing, as he described his life. Married and divorced three times, he said he was broken again and again.

I said, "When I am broken, I turn to God, and rely on my faith to get me back up again. Obviously today, you are not the person you described. Are you now a man of faith?"

He smiled and said, "On my 50th birthday, I had planned to commit suicide and had made all of the arrangements to do so. My daughter came to the house and begged me to go with her to church. I decided it would be one last good thing I could do." He never went to church and had no desire to go, but sitting in the pew, he knew the pastor was speaking directly to Him, and he gave his heart to Jesus. He told the Lord, "If you can clean me up, I will tell the world."—that was 18 years ago and he has not touched alcohol, drugs, or women since that day! Today he is a traveling evangelist who simply tells his story! We prayed for one another and I told him

I was honored to meet him, and encouraged him to keep telling his God story!

For 30-plus years I have had the great privilege of teaching and mentoring young women to know and love Jesus, to stay close to the Shepherd. I call them all my spiritual children and love them each dearly. Today, two of these precious young women, Dayna and Morgan, came to visit. I had mentored them both 10 years ago, during their college days at Texas A&M. I was thrilled to see them, and to see how they have grown and matured in their faith. Both are obviously wonderful wives and moms and both very involved in ministry work! Praise the Lord! "Therefore, my sisters, whom I love and long for, my joy and crown, stand firm thus in the Lord, my beloved." Philippians 4:1(paraphrase) God continues to bless and I look forward to tomorrow's interactions. Thank you for continued prayers for my breathing. Love you all so very much!

CHAPTER TAKEAWAY: No matter what you have done in your past, God is waiting with open arms to receive a broken and repentant heart. He desires we stay close to the Shepherd so He can protect us from the evil that would pull us away.

PERSONAL REFLECTION: Have you trusted Christ as your Savior? If so, He has covered every sin. Stay close to Him so that you are not tempted to turn away. If you fail, be quick to confess, so fellowship might be restored with your loving Father.

CHAPTER 26

WOUNDED HEARTS

May You give us a heart and passion for the culture we live in. May we not turn away from Your call. May we not shrink away from being the light that You called us to be.

Dr. Del Tackett[23]

While hospitalized, an issue came before the Supreme Court that struck a memory of wounded hearts, one being my own:

I was a single mom of two young sons when I learned I was pregnant. I held an executive position in a major corporation, and I felt certain my career would be in jeopardy if others ever found out. I had never considered

---

23 Dr. Del Tackett, *The Truth Project*, "The American Experiment: Stepping Stones."

whether or not I was "pro-choice." But at this moment, I knew I would consider the option to abort.

I adored my two sons and loved being "Mom." But I didn't stop to consider that, if I aborted, I was taking the life of perhaps another son, or maybe a daughter. I was busy with my career and busy raising my boys, and had never taken time to learn about child development in the womb, so I was quite gullible when the abortion clinic worker assured me I was not carrying a baby, but a glob of tissue. If I "took care of it," early enough, the procedure would be no different than removing a cyst. The pregnancy test revealed I was 8 weeks along. The abortion was scheduled.

The day the abortion was scheduled was a busy workday for me. I worked up until time for my appointment and read through work materials while I waited with a room full of other women. I barely listened to the "counselor" who rapidly went through consent forms, and I signed them without question. I just wanted to get the procedure over with and to leave.

I did listen when another woman, who was six months along, asked with tears streaming down her face, "Are you sure my baby won't feel any pain?" I was appalled that this woman had waited so long, until the "cyst" had become a baby. How could she let her child die?

The counselor assured her, "The 'fetus' feels no pain, and it's not a baby."

The counselor's comments, meant to reassure the woman, made me angry. In denial about the baby in my womb and the choice I had made for my child, I focused instead on the decision this woman had made regarding her child. I remembered being six months pregnant with my sons and they were breathing, and kicking and hiccupping. "How could she do this to her child?" Yet, I felt no connection or remorse for the child I was about to abort. I had convinced myself that it was only tissue, a cyst, I was removing.

I don't remember meeting the doctor prior to my procedure, but I remember the pain: intense cramping and a raw gnawing that wouldn't let up. I left following my abortion hurting physically, but feeling relieved, empowered, and ready to put that bad experience behind me.

In the year that followed I found myself defending my choice, becoming angry with those who opposed abortion. I lived in persistent denial of any connection between my abortion and the nightmares, the depression, the sense of worthlessness I was experiencing almost daily. I kept reminding myself of my career and the *better life* I could offer my two sons because of it. But I also found myself working more and more, and leaving my boys with daycare more than necessary. I still loved them deeply, but felt unworthy to be their mom.

When I learned I was pregnant, yet again, because of my promiscuous lifestyle, I confided in a friend who told me I had no choice but to abort. "It can't be wrong if it is legal," she told me.

So, once again, I made an appointment, but at a different clinic. I didn't want to face the same "counselor." I felt ashamed. When I approached the clinic, there were men and women outside carrying signs that said "Abortion kills children." I was angry that they would say such a thing, and defiantly walked passed them. I mentioned the sign to my new "counselor." She laughed and said, "Yeah, that's what they think, but the fetus is not a child, just tissue."

Once again, the clinic was full of women. This time I listened to what others were saying, and was surprised that I was not the only one coming in for a second abortion. In fact, some had had even more. I was asking if anyone else had nightmares, when the "counselor" came into the room for her presentation. I did get nods from others, meaning they too had nightmares, but the conversation was nixed.

The presentation was the same as before—assuring us the doctor would be removing a blob of tissue, nothing more; telling us it was more dangerous to carry a fetus full term, than to abort.

"But what about the nightmares, what about the depression?" I asked.

"We don't have any record of that happening, but if you want to talk to someone we can set you up with a counselor," was the reply.

I was introduced to the doctor when he entered the procedure room. He seemed to be in a hurry, and had no patience with his assistant. This time, the pain felt like a knife ripping out my insides, much worse than I had remembered before.

In the recovery room full of women, I began hemorrhaging heavily, and passed out. I woke to the doctor standing over me yelling at the assistant. He was angry, and he stormed away shouting, "Give her some juice and a cracker and don't bother me again!"

I asked the assistant if I was ok, because I didn't feel ok.

She said, "Just stay here until you feel normal." I lay there for two more hours before I felt I could drive home.

I left the abortion clinic emotionally scarred—so different from the first time. Even though my body felt recovered enough from the trauma to drive home, I felt like I had died on the inside. I cried all the way home, and into the night. True sadness, sorrow and regret engulfed me, and I hated who I had become.

I began to research the development of babies in the womb. The horrible truth about what I had done to my babies horrified me. Why was I not told that I was carrying a developing child? I had been lied to.

Nightmares of being dismembered continued, and intensified. I now made the connection between the horrible dreams and my abortions. In addition to the growing depression, I was also experiencing tremendous lower back pain. My family doctor referred me to an Ob/Gyn for examination. A hysterectomy was recommended because of damage done to my uterus. I was only 35 years old. In addition to depression and guilt, a new emotion surfaced. Anger. Anger at those who lied to me and heartlessly killed my babies.

In the years since, through heart-breaking prayer and counseling, I have made peace with God. I am thankful for my Lord and Savior Jesus Christ who has forgiven me, healed me, and restored my life.

I will live with the regret of my two abortions until the day I die, but I committed to God that I would spend the rest of my life speaking truth about the issue of abortion, so that other women would not suffer as I did. To this day, I continue in that endeavor.

I can't help but praise God that abortion was not legal in 1972. You see, that is when I learned of an out-of-wedlock pregnancy my freshman year of college. I dropped out of college, married the father of my child, and gave birth to a son on February 14, 1973—the year abortion became legal. I like to think that I would have chosen life for my son, had abortion been legal in 1972, but only God knows the bent of my heart. Jason, and my younger son, Josh, are gifts from the Lord, and it is only by God's grace that I have the privilege of being their mom.

If you have learned of an unplanned pregnancy, choose life for your child. Know that God has a purpose for you both, and will honor your life-giving decision. He will meet your every need. If you have chosen abortion in the past, agree with God that it was wrong, and receive forgiveness and healing that only He can give. Allow God to open doors of opportunity for you to minister to others who have walked in your shoes, to show them the compassion He has so graciously shown you. Tell your story, so that the next generation will not buy the lies of the enemy, as we did, regarding the sanctity of life.

June 26, 2018

The life issue, that so divides our nation politically, is actually a spiritual issue. God gives life and He numbers our days. When we decide to be our own authority, our own God, is when the enemy (Satan, the world system, and our flesh) tells us that life has no meaning, that a Designer did not create us; we evolved from apes. Believing those lies, apart from God, it is easy for man, to discard life should it become inconvenient to their future plans.

I have had two abortions. I will forever regret the decision to abort my babies. Yes, God has forgiven me, healed me, restored me, but the pain in my heart never goes away. Nor should it, as there are lifelong consequences for our choices. By God's grace, He allowed me the opportunity to direct a Pregnancy Care Center for two years. My eyes were opened to the many opportunities women have for assistance when they have an unplanned pregnancy—Opportunities to choose life for both the mother and child and, the opportunity to move forward successfully in life.

I also witnessed, time and time again, women who had had abortions coming to us for help, for counseling because of grief and other difficulties they were experiencing since their abortion— physical, mental, emotional, spiritual. It broke my heart every time to see the suffering, and I was so thankful we were prepared to help them!

I praise God every day for Pregnancy Care Centers that are all about life, not death. So today's Supreme Court decision not to force Pregnancy Care Centers to promote abortion, is a huge victory for women and their babies. I know abortion breaks God's heart. I pray it will always break ours too!

CHAPTER TAKEAWAY: Life is sacred from conception to natural death. Just because abortion is legal in our nation does not make it right in God's eyes. God is ready to offer forgiveness to those who have chosen abortion and agree with God that it was wrong. He will heal and restore the brokenhearted.

PERSONAL REFLECTION: Do you know of someone who has had an abortion? Pray they would recognize their sin, and seek forgiveness from a loving, merciful Savior.

CHAPTER 27

HIS MYSTERIOUS WAYS

God is not waiting to bless us after our troubles end. He is blessing us right now, in and through those troubles. At this exact moment, He is giving us what He thinks is good.[24]

Dr. Larry Crabb

Most every child of God has experienced His hand of blessing, provision, and protection. Occasionally, someone will tell of an unusual encounter, which he or she is certain came directly from God. Psalm 91:11 says God will *"give His angels charge over you, to keep you in all your ways."* Hebrews 14:1 says, *"Are they not all ministering spirits sent forth to minister for those who will inherit salvation?"*

---

24 Dr. Larry Crabb, *Shattered Dreams: God's Unexpected Path to Joy* (2001).

I've two encounters that I can't explain: The first, which demonstrated God's protection, occurred when I was lost and alone in my little Miata, at 9:00 PM, in Anacostia, a community of Washington D.C., not considered a safe place to be lost, even during the day. Upon leaving a television interview, I had made a wrong turn, and with no GPS or cell phone in that day, I panicked. I rolled through stop signs, afraid to stop where men were gathered on street corners. I watched desperately for a police car, but saw none. I cried out to God, "Please help me."

As I approached another stop sign, a taxi pulled up next to me. I looked over to see a silver-haired gentleman driving, not the typical description of D.C. taxi drivers. He rolled his window down and kindly asked, "You are lost, aren't you?"

I told him I was and where I was going.

He said, "Follow me, and I will take you to a familiar road."

I followed him, thanking God when I saw that familiar road. I turned on to the road and looked over to wave in appreciation, but he was gone, and nowhere in sight.

The second encounter, a ministering touch, happened one Thanksgiving. We were living in Virginia, and Bob was the pastor for the Singles Ministry at McLean Bible Church. He had around 100 older single men and women who were either divorced or widowed. Knowing that some would not have family to visit for a holiday meal, he invited those who would be alone, to join us. We learned later that an announcement had been made in church: "For those who do not have family, you are invited to the Pate's house for Thanksgiving!"

We went into high gear lining up delivery of borrowed tables and chairs, and preparing our home for an unknown number of guests. The day before, Bob was cleaning our second story windows, fell from the ladder, and broke his arm. Stress, high for both of us, brought me near a breaking point on Thanksgiving Day.

As I was cooking, Bob welcomed our guests. Some did not attend our church but heard we would welcome them, and so they came.

One such guest, Joseph, told Bob how kind and generous it was of us to open our home to others. Bob brought him to the kitchen to meet me, and Joseph immediately asked how he could help. I put him to work peeling potatoes. The entire time, he was ministering to me, telling me that everything would work out; I could relax and enjoy the day; there would be food enough for all who came. I felt better just listening to Joseph, and all that he said was correct.

We had 50 guests, filling the table settings we had prepared. And, we had a wonderful day of thanksgiving together, with an abundance of food, including dishes brought by some of the guests.

No one who attended remembers Joseph, but Bob and me. We don't know when he left or where he went, but we know God sent him.

June 23, 2018

A strange event became a God encounter! As has been the case with most meals, I was the only one in the dining room this morning at 7:00 AM. I ate my bowl of oatmeal and returned to my room with my coffee.

Ten minutes later there was a knock on my door. It was one of the cooks. She said, "Miss, you left your money on your tray, and handed me a $20 bill."

I asked her name and then said, "Francis, I didn't take money to the dining room. In fact, I have no cash with me." She insisted I come back to the table where the tray still sat.

No patients had come in the dining room since I was there. Francis pointed to the place on the tray where she found the bill, just under the edge of the bowl.

I said, "I know for certain that I did not put that money there, but God knows how it got there. He obviously wants you to have it." I shared how God has blessed us with money from unknown sources before, and we just give Him praise! So I said, "How about we just pray and thank God for this unexpected blessing in your life today!"

I prayed and tears rolled down her face. She said, "I'm going through some tough times and I guess God wants me to know that He will provide."

Amen! I look forward to conversations with Francis again, since we both experienced this God encounter!

Many of you encourage me to rest, and today was a restful day. I had a surprise visit from my dear friend Beryl and her husband Conrad, from San Antonio. Beryl's friend, Lisa, was with them. Beryl has helped me in numerous ways since I was first diagnosed with ALL, and I will be forever indebted to her.

She announced, "Lisa is going to do a concert for you!" I didn't know Lisa sang, but this explained why Beryl had been persistent in recent weeks that I send her my top favorite songs! Lisa has a beautiful voice, and sang through my song list, adding a song she had chosen.

Wow! I was overwhelmed and cried like a baby. Then the three prayed for me, and I think we all cried. I felt empowered by the Lord following my friends' visit. The Lord must be preparing me for a big week!

My breathing and coughing are much improved! My surgery wound is healing nicely, so please pray my 10-day stay will be cut to 7! Bless you all for your love, encouragement, and prayers!

CHAPTER TAKEAWAY: God's ways are not our ways. We know there are ministering angels among us, but only God knows what He sends them to do on behalf of the saints. We don't have to have all of the answers or be able to explain when we know God has intervened with supernatural help. But we should always give Him praise!

PERSONAL REFLECTION: Perhaps you have encountered God's helping hand under mysterious circumstances. Take time to thank Him and praise Him for His intervention.

CHAPTER 28

OUR HOPE IS IN CHRIST

To the degree that this life is viewed as a place of pilgrimage—a place where it is never honorable or right to build a lasting foundation—I am released to live and love through seeing my life used to advance your progress and joy in Christ.

Dan Allender

Losing a loved one is excruciatingly difficult. Our finite minds want to understand why God took them away too soon. Our grief may lead us to lash out at God in anger, assuming He acted cruelly toward our loved one by allowing them to die, and cruelly toward us by leaving us to live without them. If only we could see the bigger picture.

For those who know Christ, going Home is truly a glorious experience. They are celebrating! For those left behind, although the grief is real, the separation is temporary. We know the reunion one day will be for eternity.

I made a point to talk with my family, including my grandchildren, about my possible "Homegoing." I wanted them each to know that I was ready to see Jesus, and to be healed completely. I shared how I look forward to seeing our loved ones who are already with Jesus. I assured them that if God chose to take me, it would be a temporary separation, because one day we will all be together again, and would never ever be apart.

As a follow-up to my talk with family, I realized my memorial celebration needed to reflect the same excitement and joy that I had conveyed to them. So my dear friend, Tammie, helped me plan a "Homegoing Celebration." I am donating my body to medical research, so there will be no body, no casket. An uplifting memorial will include upbeat music and a message of hope for all attending. But the best part will follow the service—an ice cream social including a buffet of assorted ice cream and toppings! Now that is the way to celebrate a resurrection!

June 24, 2018

"How do you praise God in the storm?" That was the question Maria had as she was cleaning my room this morning.

I was listening to the song, "Praise Him in the Storm," by Casting Crowns. I told her that the storm is temporary; this life and all we have is temporary; and I am certain I will spend eternity with my Savior where there is no more pain and suffering.

Maria said she was a believer but struggled with trusting and praising God after her younger brother died of cancer. She said he was also a believer, and his death did not make sense to her. She grieves daily.

I told her how very sorry I was to hear of her brother's passing. I said, "You know Maria, God grieves for your loss too! He hates what sin has done to this world. He created a paradise for mankind with no sin. He gave man free will, because He loved man and wanted love in return that wasn't forced. But Adam and Eve believed the lies of the enemy, and pride caused them to reject the authority of God. So in His perfection He had to cast them out of Eden and creation was cursed. The seed of sin through Adam is in every human being, but we have free will to love God and accept His plan for salvation in Christ, or to reject His authority and determine to be our own god. But the result of that latter route is spiritual death—separation from God for eternity. As more and more reject God, we see more and more evil, pain, suffering, chaos and loss in this fallen world.

But the good news is that Christ will return to make all things right again! I regularly pray 'Come Lord Jesus!'"

I told Maria she could have the joy of knowing that when God takes her Home, she will see her brother again, and will be with him for eternity, never to be separated again. With tears, she said, "Really?"

I shared 1 Thessalonians 4: 14, 16-17, "For if we believe that Jesus died and rose again, even so God will bring with Him those who sleep in Jesus. For the Lord Himself will descend from heaven with a shout, with the voice of an archangel, and with the trumpet of God. And the dead in Christ will rise first. Then we who are alive and remain shall be caught up together with them in the clouds to meet the Lord in the air. And thus we shall always be with the Lord."

Maria said she had never read that. I shared other passages that she wrote down to encourage her grieving heart. Pray for Maria in her loss, that she will have the joy and hope of Christ's promises.

I am improving daily, and by God's grace I hope to be home in a few days! Your prayers are certainly being answered. Thank you!

CHAPTER TAKEAWAY: Because we live in a cursed world, everyone will die a physical death. All will be raised to life, but only those who have trusted Christ as their Savior will spend eternity with Him. Those who reject Christ will spend eternity separated, from God, and from those who believed in Him.

PERSONAL REFLECTION: Do you recognize the importance of trusting Christ as your Savior and telling others the good news of salvation? Have you thanked God for the hope you have in Christ, to be reunited for eternity with all loved ones who believe?

CHAPTER 29

WE ARE FAMILY

I always thank my God when I pray for you, because I keep hearing about your faith in the Lord Jesus and your love for all of God's people. And I am praying that you will put into action the generosity that comes from your faith as you understand and experience all the good things we have in Christ. Your love has given me much joy and comfort, my brother, for your kindness has often refreshed the hearts of God's people.

Philemon 4-7(NLT)

I have been blessed with incredible blood relatives. My mother had eight sisters and two brothers. One brother and sister died as infants, but I had the privilege of being raised among the remaining aunts, uncles and cousins. My dad was the youngest of seven children. I was blessed to know two of his sisters and one brother, as well as their children and grandkids.

In our family, most holidays were celebrated at the home of my grandmother, on my Mother's side. She made every person feel as though they were her favorite. Even those outside of the family affectionately called her "Mom." Mom's three younger daughters were like sisters to me, just stairsteps above me in age. Many of my best childhood memories revolve around Jo, Judy, and Becky.

I spent most of my weekends as a teen at Mom's house. I loved being near my precious grandmother, and always wanted to be like her: always putting others first, and loving others unconditionally. She and her sister Velear poured so much love into my life and into my children's lives. Their godly example made a lasting impact. That's what family does.

My earthly family provides a tiny glimpse of how beautiful it is to also be a part of the family of God. When you meet another believer, one who shares your love of Christ and others, you meet a kindred spirit. It is a spirit of commonality, acceptance, love and joy. You never feel alone when you are with spiritual family. even when you are confined to a hospital.

June 25, 2018

Have you met someone and within minutes thought, "I'll bet they love Jesus?" When someone is a believer, and walks daily with Jesus— seeking to know Him and to love Him more, it is evident in their behavior. The overflow of love, joy, peace, patience, kindness, etc., is very different than what you see in an unbeliever, or even in a believer who does not walk closely with God. It is supernatural.

The Holy Spirit speaks to your spirit and you just know you are meeting a brother or sister in Christ.

Such is the case with Bianca, my night nurse over the weekend. She would come into the room with such joy and peace in her demeanor. Within minutes we were talking about our faithful and loving Savior. She shared that during the week she is a Hospice nurse. It is her calling from God. She is passionate about ministering and caring for those about to meet their Maker. She said she has freedom where she works to pray with the patients, their families, and help them to know about Jesus. She said it is such a blessing to see a patient find assurance of salvation in Christ before they pass, and to see the peace they have, knowing they will live for eternity with Him.

Bianca and I bonded immediately, exchanged contact information, and promised to stay in touch. That is what family does.

Elizabeth is a CNA, with such a servant's heart. She just can't do enough for you. I told her she was spoiling me. Elizabeth is from Nigeria, and like Bianca, I knew without a doubt that she loved Jesus. In fact she often says, "Thank you Jesus," spontaneously in conversation. She believed in the saving work of Jesus while in Nigeria, hearing a missionary speak. She said she just couldn't get enough of God.

She said, "I pray and read my Bible, because I love Him so much. He has been very good to me and I don't deserve it." I told her that none of us do. That is what is so amazing about grace! I had the joy of praying with her and she prayed for me. That is what family does!

I do have much to tell about my health, and it is good, but please bear with me until Bob and I talk to the doctors on July 3rd to confirm long-term plans. Then I will share an incredible God-story, of which you have all been a part. I wish I could hug each of you and look you in the eyes to show my appreciation! One day we will! That is what family does!

CHAPTER TAKEAWAY: There is tremendous joy experienced when two believers meet and share their common bond of love for their Savior. I believe it is God's nudging of our spirits to know without a doubt that we are talking to another believer.

PERSONAL REFLECTION: Have you met a stranger, but knew in your spirit that they must be a fellow believer in Christ? Thank God that He gives us that knowledge and for the commonality we share which brings such joy.

CHAPTER 30

GOD STILL PERFORMS MIRACLES

It is a wonderful thing to be on the mountaintop with God, but a person only gets there so he may later go down and lift up the people in the valley. The true test of our spiritual life is in exhibiting the power to descend from the mountain.

Oswald Chambers

When my prognosis was very much in question, I wanted to follow the teaching of James 5:14 for the sick: to call for the elders of the church, and let them pray over me, anointing me with oil in the name of the Lord. I asked Dr. Dave Anderson, President of Grace School of Theology, who is also a former pastor, church planter, and a dear spiritual mentor and friend. I also asked Dan Greer, Pastor of Community Baptist Church in the Woodlands, TX, a church family we had grown to love in the previous year through their prayers, visits and support.

These two men graciously responded and visited me in the hospital to pray over me. Dr. Anderson asked me what I understood about this passage, in regard to my desire for healing. I told him that I know God can heal me if He chooses. That to me is the faith factor. But I understand that He may not choose to do so.

God knows what is best for me. He also knows how He might receive the most glory—whether in my life, or in my death. My asking for prayer as James suggests, is my telling God, "I believe You can heal me, but Your will be done." Dr. Anderson said my understanding was correct, and the two men prayed fervently for me.

I knew that if the Lord chose to heal me this side of heaven, that it is not a permanent situation. My physical body will die, and so will yours. If we are blessed to receive an extension in the life of our earthly bodies, it is for God's purposes. We are wise to seek Him and to be obedient to all that He asks of us in the additional days we are given. We are all passing through and preparing for eternity. When I stand before Jesus Christ, I want to hear Him say, "Well done, my good and faithful servant." Each day is an opportunity to fulfill my calling and to finish well, in His strength.

July 3, 2018

Prayer warrior praises: Let me start by saying thank you for praying for Bob and me so faithfully over these past three years! We could not have made it without your unfailing love and support. I was in remission within a few months following my Bone Marrow Transplant in February of 2017. But because my donor's marrow and blood cells did not take over, 100%, there was a likelihood that I would relapse. That percentage continued to drop and my abnormal cells continued to grow in number. And finally, I did relapse around 7 weeks ago. The doctor told me the Leukemia had returned aggressively and it would have to be attacked aggressively, hence the full week of Chemo and 4 weeks of recovery in the hospital.

Quite frankly, I am still recovering. Awaiting results of a lumbar puncture and bone marrow biopsy, the doctors explained again that there needed to be a trace of cancer in order to get the CarT cell therapy (a therapy that has many risks and has only been successful with patients under 29 years of age). If I am in remission, I would immediately start regular rounds of Chemo and continue daily oral chemo, to keep Leukemia from returning aggressively again.

I thought about the past 2 1/2 years living with a compromised immune system: keeping me from family and friends, public places, and from teaching, speaking, doing the things I know God has called me to do.

So, I told Bob, "I've decided not to do anymore Chemo. I'm tired. You are tired. I'm done." He gave me his full support but reminded me of how God's hand was over our coming to Houston, and getting me to Methodist Hospital in those early days. He suggested I might want to ask God for direction.

By this time, I was in the Transition Center, which God amazingly had provided for my recovery. I prayed all through the night for wisdom regarding what I should do. I confessed that I was trying to control my future, rather than continuing to trust God's good plan. I confessed my doubt that God would use Chemo to heal me.

The next morning I was reading, again, the book, Maximum Joy, by Dr. Dave Anderson. In the book he tells a personal story about concern for blood clots and a greater concern for taking Coumadin. I read his statement:

"They all (doctors) agreed that the risk of blood clots was greater than the risk of well monitored use of Coumadin, for a brief period of time, to keep the clots from forming."

With my pen, and without really thinking, I marked out "blood clots" and wrote, "relapse;"

I marked out "Coumadin" and wrote, "Chemo;"

I marked out "clots" and wrote, "cancer!"

It now read, "They all agreed that the risk of relapse was greater than the risk of well-monitored Chemo, for a brief period of time, to keep the cancer from forming."

Wow! I had no doubt that God was speaking to my heart. I wasn't sure what to think of it though. I turned the page, literally, and the phone rang. It was my oncologist.

Get this: He said "I have amazing news. Your Bone Marrow Biopsy was completely clear; there are no abnormal cells; your Donor Marrow percentage is 100%. You are in complete remission! We are very surprised. We can't explain how your donor cell percentage went to 100 after aggressive Chemo. We have never seen that before."

I said, "It is answered prayer, Dr. Pingali. So, no more chemo?"

He said "You must come in for another week of Chemo, but a lighter dosage. We will discuss all of this with you and Bob on July 3rd."

Well, today, when the doctor entered the room he had a big smile. He couldn't wait to show me the reports so I could see for myself: FULL REMISSION, ZERO ABNORMAL CELLS, 100% DONOR CELLS!! He said, "After consideration, we have decided you don't have to be admitted to hospital for more chemo. Continue taking the daily oral chemo (very minimal side effects) and we will monitor your blood monthly for any changes!"

We are praising the Lord for His faithfulness, His goodness, and for giving me hope for more days to serve Him and to enjoy my family! We praise Him for urging His children to pray for us, and for your obedience to His leading, and for your love for us! We can't thank you enough this side of heaven! Please know that Bob and I love each of you! We look forward to telling our story again and again to give God all the glory!

CHAPTER TAKEAWAY: God still performs miracles. God still heals. He is God and nothing is impossible with Him. But should He choose not to heal, He is still good and perfect in all of His ways. We will understand it all when we see Christ face to face.

PERSONAL TAKEAWAY: Have you grasped the power of our God, and the power of prayer in your battles? More importantly, do you understand the depths of His love and goodness towards you? Ask God to help you see Him as He is, to help you trust His good plan for your life.

CHAPTER 31

THE THANK-YOU LIFE

The pressure of hard places makes us value life. Every time our life is given back to us from such a trial, it is like a new beginning, and we learn better how much it is worth, and make more of it for God and man.

A.B. Simpson[25]

As of this writing, it has been seven months since I received the good news of my complete remission. I continue to gain strength and become healthier each day. I have returned to a more normal daily routine, and to the ministry I love. God has nudged me to write this book, and He is enabling me to complete it for His good purposes. In the midst of this book project my mother went Home to be with Jesus, after a two-year battle with

---

25 A.B. Simpson, quote from a selection in *Streams in the Desert*.

congestive heart failure and other complications that come with aging. Her passing was just another reminder of the sting of death, but oh the hope we have in Christ Jesus! I know I will see Mother and Dad again one day, never to be separated again.

As I have said, only God knows the number of our days and I don't want to waste a day of His mercy and grace over my life. All that I am and have belongs to Him. I am so grateful for the understanding of God's grace and the abundant life that He gives us.

Bob and I both trusted Christ as our Savior when we were children, but we lacked the biblical understanding of the fact that Christ's love can never be earned and can never be lost. All we knew were the supposed *rules* of how to live the Christian life. We lived what Dr. Dave Anderson describes as a *"have to"* life.

Maybe you can relate to the feeling of duty, trying hard to earn God's acceptance and love to gain assurance of heaven when you die. Or perhaps like us, the continuous effort to prove to yourself, and to others watching, that you are indeed a Christian.

For Bob and me, it was exhausting, causing doubt about our ability to live the Christian life. And to be frank, living trying to get on God's "accepted" list was quite hypocritical and offensive to God: *Have I done the right things? Have I done enough? Which behavior earns the spot of proving to others that I am a Christian?*

Notice that kind of thinking is all about what I do, not what Christ has already done on my behalf. Our failed attempts and frustration in *trying hard* to live the Christian life, led both of us to walk away from the church in our early days as believers. We lost interest in Christian fellowship and God's Word. For a number of years, we both chased worldly pursuits—our careers, money and all that money could buy, for happiness and success.

Dr. Larry Moyer of *EvanTell* says there are three types of people in the world who want to go to heaven:

1. Those who say you can go to heaven by being good. But if that is true, says Moyer, then Christ didn't have to die, did he?

2. Those who think you have to believe in Jesus, but also have to live a good life. But if that is true, then Jesus did not do enough, did He?

3. Those who believe Jesus paid it all.[26]

Believing Jesus "paid it all" opened the windows of heaven for us to now live a *thank you* life. Each morning we look forward to getting into His Word, with a hunger and desire to know Him more intimately, and to prepare our hearts and minds for the day ahead.

We are in awe of this Jesus who loves us and is transforming us into His image as we stay close to Him. We pray together about being available for all that the Lord asks us to do. We get excited about the opportunities He brings our way through daily interactions with people.

At the end of the day we rejoice over the stories we share with one another, all about God's amazing grace working through us, to love others and to point them to Christ. We fall in love with Jesus all over again, every single day.

---

26 R. Larry Moyer, *101 Tips for Evangelism: Practical Ways to Enhance Your Witness* (Hendrickson, 2017).

Inevitable, continual failures break our hearts. We are thankful for 1 John 1:9 which promises that if we confess our sins, He is faithful to forgive us and to cleanse us from all unrighteousness. God restores fellowship and intimacy with Him.

Our relationship when we fail is never in jeopardy, as Christ paid the price for all of our sins, past, present, and future, on the cross. His Holy Spirit in us, since the moment we believed, guarantees our relationship with the Father for eternity.

Christ desires to live the abundant life through us as we desire Him more fully in our lives. This full and joyful life compels us to share Christ's love and grace with all who will hear. Wouldn't you share the best thing that has ever happened in your daily Christian life, with others?

How can you enjoy the abundant, thank-you life?

Simply place your trust in Christ alone, for forgiveness of sins and eternal life with Him. Watch Him reveal His amazing strength and power through you, to touch others, even in your weakest days. Open your eyes to the world around you, and recognize how God has equipped you to live with purpose and joy. Begin your glorious adventure with God today!

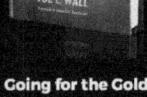